Praise for
Life with "Doc"

Reading this book, *Life with "Doc": My Husband & My Teacher, Dr. David R. Hawkins,* I felt as if I were living with HIM and going through the learning experiences which Susan went through! She brings HIM alive to be your companion to walk with you through all of life's situations…. The author and the book connect us with the Divine Spirit that is everywhere, helping us in our aspiration to attain higher levels of spiritual evolution.

— **Swami Chidatmananda**
Hindu monk, Chinmaya Mission, Hyderabad, India

LIFE WITH "DOC":
My Husband & My Teacher, Dr. David R. Hawkins

Susan Hawkins

Veritas Publishing
2022

Cataloging-in-Publication Data is on file
at the Library of Congress

Tradepaper ISBN: 978-1-7333764-4-0
E-book ISBN: 978-1-7333764-5-7
10 9 8 7 6 5 4 3 2 1
1st edition, September 2022
Printed in the United States of America

Dedicated to the students of Dr. Hawkins's work.

Straight is the path and narrow is the way. Waste no time!

—Dr. David R. Hawkins

CONTENTS

PREFACE

David and I met in country-western dance class and never stopped dancing together. We danced in parking lots, grocery stores, restaurants, and doctors' offices! Even after his passing, our dance continues as I carry on the work that he left for me to do. I am not alone because his essence is inside of me.

I knew when I met him that his love and wisdom were so great that I had to share him with the rest of the world. I couldn't just keep him to myself. And Dave was always willing to share himself with anyone who was sincerely interested in what he had to share.

We were a good match—we fit together like a glove on the hand. We knew we had a commitment to share what he was with the world. This book is yet another expression of our commitment.

He told me that, one day, I would need to write something of my own journey and what it was like to live with him. To that end, during the last few years, I have recorded my memories and put them into this book for you.

Dave taught me that it's our duty to give back what we have been given, whether it's for one person or for many. I'm grateful for my life with him. And I'm grateful for all of you who bring your spirit and love to our work.

This book is my way of giving something back. I hope and pray you find it helpful for your journey. As he taught us: "Straight is the path, and narrow is the way. Waste no time!"

—Susan Hawkins, Sedona, Arizona

FOREWORD

Reading this book, *Life with "Doc": My Husband & My Teacher, Dr. David R. Hawkins*. I felt as if I were living with HIM and going through the learning experiences that Susan went through! She brings HIM alive to be your companion to walk with you through all of life's situations.

The book reveals to us about the Divine Light-Divine Energy that appeared to Susan, which made them start the spiritual work of writing books and giving lectures for the sake of providing Higher Guidance to spiritual seekers in the world.

The combination of both of them is like the Spirit (Purusha) and the Nature (Prakriti) coming together in order to bring about the most beautiful manifestations of this Creation (Existence).

Susan's spiritual experiences and universal outlook towards all religions are quite inspiring. The fact that they were together in 12 lifetimes (including this life) presents to us how Divine ordinance brought them together with perfect synchronicity for providing the Higher Spiritual pathway for people to walk with confidence and ease.

The practical experience that she describes of Doc letting go of all resistance to pain, surrendering his personal will to Divinity, and thereby attaining a state of ecstasy to remain close to the heart of God during his surgery with no anesthesia, leaves us in awe and wonder as to how Doc could attain such a state while under the knife.

How their marriage came about for the sake of helping Doc to function in this world by coming out of his divine states of consciousness, so that he could provide rare guidance to spiritual seekers, tells us about the Sanctity of it.

Through Susan, we come to know that Doc let people be what they were. He always lived by the principle of attraction and not promotion. He recommended contemplation, where you carry your spiritual awareness with you at all times, in the background, while you are going through your day.

Doc was always in prayer, asking for knowledge of God's will for his life and the power to carry it out. "Live your life like a prayer" is one of his teachings. For Doc, in his daily life, it meant surrendering everything to God. The bottom line of prayer is to turn your whole life over to God.

Susan describes how he handled negative people. If negativity continued even after giving them many chances, he did not retaliate, but just walked away from the relationship, leaving it to karma to handle the situation.

Describing the Higher State that Doc was in, Susan says that he was everywhere, in everything—that was his perspective. "There is only one Self," he said, and he saw the Self radiating from everyone and everything. He didn't see separateness; he saw Allness.

His humility of being a Divine channel is depicted when he says that he himself did not perform the miracles. Divinity just used his aura as a conduit for healing energy to be poured out to others when needed.

She describes how they used kinesiology (muscle-testing) for saying only the Truth, because he did not want the karma of saying or writing something that wasn't true. Readers of their books are exposed only to the Truth, as everything that is mentioned therein is nothing but Truth.

In this book, one discovers the most precious advice for spiritual seekers: avoiding traps of money, sex and fame by knowing that whatever loving energy we have, it is not personal but Divine.

Their shared experience of facing death while travelling in the plane, teaches us how to be spiritually prepared for death by believing in God and knowing the peace and security present in our Soul.

Through this book, we come to learn the essence of unconditional love. When you love people, you let them go, and you let them live their own life. You want them to grow. You don't cling or tell them what to do. That's the essence of the teaching on unconditional love.

Susan shares with us what Doc did during his last days in the body by spending most of the time in prayer to be loving toward all things at all times. She also tells us how HE handled the betrayal from trusted ones by accepting it as God's will and surrendering it to God and letting karma handle it.

What did Doc want for his followers? Susan shares with us that he wanted us to focus on our own consciousness, to make sure his teaching enters our own heart so that we are transformed. This requires constant devotion to our inner work. He was not interested in promoting his work; he said his teaching will go where it needs to go when the time is ready for it to go there.

Susan experiences the Presence of Doc whenever needed. This tells us the perfect tuning of her heart and soul with Doc and her inner levels of Purity. She says, "He told us that he would continue to be here and be available as a vibration within the collective consciousness. He also said that if you focus on his energy in your mind and heart, then he is present with you. I find that to be very true. Whenever I need him, he is here."

Susan lives his teaching, "Just do the good and let it go." She does her best in doing something kind without needing a reward or recognition. She says, "We plant the seeds but let go of the results." It's good when we can do our jobs or our work around the house or in society and not need to be in the limelight with it. Or get a reward for it. She sincerely follows what Doc did; he did everything, not for any reward, but only for the fulfillment of knowing he had done his part to help mankind.

Simple kindness to oneself, and all that lives, is the most powerful transformational force of all, and Susan practices by living this teaching. Her living itself is a silent teaching for all of us to imbibe.

This book guides us into the practice of contemplation. Susan says that contemplation is something that Doc did all the time. He taught that meditation can be helpful. You learn how to focus your attention and go within to explore various inner states. For many decades, he meditated for an hour in the morning and an hour in the evening. But, Doc said, meditation has limited value because it is compartmentalized from the rest of your life, so he recommended contemplation and Susan tells us his constancy with it: "I saw him do this, nonstop. Whatever he was doing, he had an inner awareness of God in the background. I would see him sit quietly, inwardly contemplating."

This book gives us guidance regarding our prayers for the sake of others. We can pray for their highest good, out of our love for them, and that absolutely brings the Light of God's Grace to help them.

Susan has no fear of the future because Doc said that consciousness is always evolving. Things are always changing. Creation and destruction are both innate to the circle of life. Civilizations come and go, but consciousness is always evolving.

Susan assures us about HIS presence, "His body is ash, but his Spirit is everywhere." The author and the book connect us with the Divine Spirit, which is everywhere, helping us in our aspiration to attain higher levels of spiritual evolution.

—Swami Chidatmananda, Hyderabad, India

INTRODUCTION

The first time I saw Susan Hawkins, she was on stage. I had just read *Power vs. Force: Hidden Determinants of Human Behavior* and was eager to hear the author, Dr. David R. Hawkins, so I signed up for one of his lectures.

When the event began, I was surprised to see his wife on stage with him, but the significance of her presence was immediately obvious. Throughout the lecture, Dr. Hawkins looked at her often—as if she were his landmark on stage. He walked over to her to use her arm for muscle-testing various statements. They were a single unit, moving in tandem; where he left off, she began, and vice versa. They seemed to communicate silently (telepathically) with each other throughout the lecture. At the end, he motioned for her to stand with him as he gave a final blessing for the audience. He held onto her arm to steady himself. After the standing ovation, she gently guided him off stage.

It was obvious to me that the body of work had come through them, *together*. Doc was the official "author," and Susan the "right arm." He often said, "She was the fulcrum that made it possible." A year after that lecture, he wrote of her contributions in the Acknowledgments of his book, *Truth vs. Falsehood*:

> It has also been my good fortune to have at my side a wonderful wife, co-worker, and helpmate, Susan, who has been a mainstay of research as well as an associate at the many lecture presentations. She did over 7,000 calibrations for just this work alone, plus thousands of others devoted to intensive research projects around the clock, seven days a week, for years. Her own one-on-one teaching has been warmly received by the many hundreds who have experienced her warmth and personal interest.

Neither of them, however, ever claimed personal credit for the body of work that came through them. They both viewed Divinity as the Source, and themselves merely as the channel of the teachings, which is why they began every lecture by stating, *"Gloria in Excelsis Deo!"* Doc wrote at the beginning of his book, *Truth vs. Falsehood*: "All gratitude is due to the inspiration of the Presence of Divinity whose effulgence radiates forth to the world as the All-Present Eternal Source of All that Exists, the formless out of which form is the actualized Infinite Potentiality of the ongoingness of Creation."

Susan Hawkins—Behind the Scenes

As you'll see in this book, Susan is down-to-earth and has a big heart. The first time I met with her and Doc, they invited me out to lunch to discuss a letter I had written to them. At the lunch, I was trying to act properly pious. After all, this was my spiritual teacher and his wife, and I wanted to impress them! Within the first five minutes, Susan's earthy humor undid my pretension. I was suddenly belly-laughing as she told a funny story about pigs from her years growing up on a farm. She said, "I'm a farm girl from the Midwest. We tell it like it is." That was in 2006, and we have at least one good belly laugh every time we talk.

She was indispensable to Doc. Over the years, going to their home, I saw firsthand that she was his "right arm" in every way. She was his co-worker, lovemate, spiritual companion, emotional comfort, protector, business manager, and physical caretaker all at once. When I was there to work with Doc on a book project, he always paused our work as soon as Susan came back from her many tasks. He lit up in her presence and was delighted to hear about her trip into town or wherever she had been. One time, she had gone up on the roof to clean out the gutters! She is an energetic woman of many talents—unafraid to get her hands dirty, yet equally at home on stage or dining with dignitaries.

Most importantly, she understood her husband's inner workings. Whenever Doc was dealing with any kind of inner difficulty, she sensed it immediately and helped him to detect the energy block that needed to be addressed. One time, for example, he was beset by negative energies coming from the collective. He was preparing his lecture on Love (2011), and it was bringing up the opposite of love (hostility, malice). It was causing him intense physical pain, and he called out to Susan. I watched with amazement as she helped him get to the core of it through dialogue and muscle-testing. She was compassionate toward his suffering, and she was able to use her keen intuition to help him resolve the inner struggle. They shared a rare intimacy on the inner level that allowed them to support each other's deepest commitments. In this book, for example, you will read her account of being in South Korea and how she helped him find relief from the intensely painful physical experience of "crushing bones" that accompanies a certain very high state.

At their May 2011 lecture, Doc said: "That's the commitment you make when you get married, to be there when the other person goes through such anguishes. The only concern I have about it is that it will be distressing to you." Susan replied, "Well, it isn't an easy thing to watch…but it's who you are and what your commitments are…you actually carry the weight of negative things."

On stage, she helped him endure. During that same lecture, Doc turned his arm toward Susan and whispered, "Bless that and pray for it, honey. My arm. A pain and weakness I've never had it before. We ask for Thy blessing and a miracle on this left arm. Amen." A few minutes later, he whispered to her, "It's better now."

I have never seen a couple so united in purpose. They each had their own personalities and talents, but they worked in tandem. Susan shares in this book about the respect they had for each other, and I got to witness that mutual respect every time I was at their home. Her purpose in all that she did was to help Doc fulfill his responsibility to God and humanity. Alongside this serious commitment, their home life was full of laughter and affection. They were easily playful and had a great sense of humor together. There was nothing uptight or pious about them.

They spoke about their marriage at the lecture on "The Mystic" (December 2007), in response to the question, "Can you speak to the challenges to love someone on the path when they are a mystic?" Doc responded: "There's a mutual adoration of the Divinity within each other, and a commitment to go through with the other person, and a fulfillment of potentiality. The fact that there might be a wrinkle in the sheet that bothers her when she sleeps means I have to straighten it … both of us are vertical, not just horizontal. We want whatever makes each other happiest."

Susan has a big heart. Recently, we went out for breakfast. When the waitress found out it was Susan Hawkins at the table, her eyes got big and she exclaimed, "Oh Susan Hawkins!" I thought that maybe the waitress was a fan of Dr. Hawkins and recognized Susan from stage or internet videos. Instead, she said, "I've heard all about you from Aunt Rose. Our whole family is grateful to you. If it weren't for you, I don't know what we'd do." The waitress went on to explain that Susan had been helping care for her aunt, who is elderly and sick and struggling to make ends meet. This family knows nothing about Susan as a public figure, wife of Dr. David Hawkins. They know her as she is: a generous and loving person.

Doc himself described Susan as "devoted without spiritual ambition." This is what he said—as you will read in the dialogue at the end of this Introduction—one day when I was at their house to work with him on a project: "Susan doesn't have spiritual ambition." I think that you, sincere readers, will agree with me that this is a rare quality. Most seekers I know (including myself!) have at least a little "spiritual ambition," wanting to "progress" or "attain" to some "higher" level. It can be so subtle, that secret wanting something for one's own self.

Here's an example. Susan and I recently visited the Amitabha Stupa, a Buddhist meditation garden with prayer wheels and a walking path. Susan saw a beautiful white feather on the ground and said, "That's when you know an angel is watching over you."

To be honest with you, I was thinking to myself, *What an auspicious sign! I'd like to take it home and put it on my altar!* To my surprise, Susan picked up the feather and said, "Let's walk back over to the Stupa and put it down as an offering." This touched me very much. I had been thinking of my own spiritual benefit, but she was thinking *beyond herself*, to offer what she had been given to the greater good. This is Susan's nature. She's not in it for herself, but for the sake of God and others.

One day I asked her, "Wasn't it hard to share your husband with thousands of other people?" She said, "There was no other way. It was his destiny. I loved him, and this meant I had to share him." Her statement made a big impression on me. How many of us would be willing to share our lovemate with the rest of the world?

The Significance of this Book

This book is yet another way that Susan is sharing Doc with us. As far as I know, Susan's book is unique in spiritual literature. Of all the great accounts about mystics and saints, I've never come across any book like this, which is a first-hand account of what it was like to *live with* a mystic as a lovemate. As Doc said in the dialogue below: "She's an inside observer."

Doc tells us that the state of the mystic is a state of consciousness beyond personhood, for in that state, there is no longer a "me." It is a state of "Revelation" in which one is transfigured, motionless, and wordless. There is no "me" that is separate from "you." Though people refer to the "mystic" as a person, there's actually no person left. It has been dissolved, annihilated, erased, transcended. To use a famous metaphor from mystical literature, the self has dissolved into God "like sugar into warm water."

"Most mystics retire from society," he tells us. I mean, how *would* you function in the world if you couldn't distinguish between yourself and other people? Through great effort, and to fulfill a karmic responsibility, Doc says, a few mystics are able to return to the world, to "write and teach about the rare state that lies beyond the dualities of the ego and its identification with form." We can think of a few famous ones from history, such as Meister Eckhart, Ramakrishna, Hildegard, Teresa of Avila, Ibn Arabi, and the like.

Most of the mystics that we know about from history were celibate monastics who did not have a family life. Thus, we do not have an account, of which I am aware, about a mystic from the viewpoint of their lovemate. "Lovemate" is the word that Doc often used to describe Susan, that special person with whom one is intimate on every level.

Therefore, Susan's book makes an invaluable contribution not only to students of Dr. Hawkins' path of Devotional Nonduality, but also to the larger repository of spiritual literature worldwide.

Dialogue with Doc and Susan

This Introduction includes a transcript of a dialogue that took place with Doc and Susan at their home in 2008. I had gone there to interview him for a biography, and then Susan walked in to see if we wanted anything to drink. She ended up sitting down and sharing some of her own experiences. After that, I asked to interview her about her life. Soon after the interviews, I gave the dialogue transcripts to Doc and Susan to review, which they did. Within a week, they both returned their transcripts and gave their approval for the dialogue to be published. Here are the pertinent excerpts...

August 4, 2008

Meeting with Doc in his little office at home. Susan walks in after her errands in town. He is delighted to see her and includes her in our conversation. It was completely spontaneous.

Doc: We were just talking about the shift from a mystic to a formal teacher, from living by yourself and you realize the full truth of something and then emerge back into the world in a formal teaching mode.

Susan: Yes, he had to re-learn how to walk and talk and recognize people.

Fran: And you (Susan) were a big part of that?

Doc: Without her, I couldn't have done it.

Susan: It is true.

Doc: She was my enabler and, without her, it would have been impossible.

Susan: It's just that he was telling me all this stuff, and I said, "David, why are you sitting on this?" And I said, "You've got to write a book on this! This is really interesting! Why are you sitting on all this information and not writing a book on it?" And then came *Power vs Force*.

Doc: So, she dragged me back into the world by my hair—with me resisting all the way! And she did it by reminding me of my responsibility. So, she got me in my Achilles' heel.

Susan: I told him, "It's your responsibility as a teacher basically to share this information, not just sit on it."

Doc: So, she had me!

Susan: I said, "Why are you just sitting on it? What good is that going to do anybody?"

Doc: So, she was my fulcrum of re-emergence into the world. She was the fulcrum.

Susan: Well, it's kind of like having the answer to cancer and not using it. It's for the benefit of mankind. That's how I was looking at it.

....

Susan: What's really challenging is when… Where were we? You kept going into high states. It was recently. All of a sudden. When Dave goes into a high state, he just kind of stands there, with this blank look, like, "Oh I've been here before…" And his eyes look glassed over. Glassed over.

You can't move him, and you can't talk to him. And you just stand there, and you say, "We're in the middle of something, you gotta move!" So literally I have to grab him by his hand and take him. All of a sudden, he'll look at something or somebody and pick up their essence, and then he's gone. It's just that I have to watch for those times!

Doc: She wants to make sure she doesn't lose me.

Fran: I remember one time at your lecture, it seemed like you were going to die. You were in a high state and started to walk down the aisle. You, Susan, started to cry...

Susan: Yeah, he said he was given the choice on whether to leave or not leave. That was a hard lecture to get through. You don't know when that state is going to come in and take over. Sometimes when he speaks... you know... it's hard for me sometimes. I'm afraid he's going to bliss out and not be able to talk any more, or that will be the end of the lecture. And that's what he was afraid of too, I think. When you first started speaking, weren't you afraid that you'd just go into that high state and bliss out?

Doc: Yes, because if you talk of the state, it tends to bring it back more forcefully. And you're never sure you're gonna make it through to the end or not. The world cares about the body, you see. And I have to remember that the world cares about that.

Susan: About this person, this physical being.

Doc: Yeah, if I laid out on the floor to leave, the world would be upset, so in deference to the world, you get up and walk on if you can. I don't know why. Divine ordinance, I guess.

....

Susan: People don't know this, but I had a really high experience before we even started in on all this. It was early morning, around 4 a.m., and Dave and I were lying in bed. All of a sudden, I looked at the corner of the room and there was a Light that got bigger and bigger until it came into the whole room. It was the most brilliant Light you could think of. My eyes were wide-open. And if you closed your eyes, you could see and feel this Light. Then suddenly the Light went into me. There was an Energy with that Light. It was engulfing. I asked Dave what it was, and he said, "Divine Light." It changed me.

Doc: Divine Light, yes.

Susan: Divine Light came in and *that* is when we started the work. That's when we really started the work. That's when we started doing the lectures. Why I had to have that experience, I don't know. It was in 1998. And it was the most unusual experience I have ever had. After that, I knew we had to start the work.

Doc: That's what Bill Wilson had. The room lit up. It was lit up by the Presence. Which is not different from Light, which is not different from Love.

Susan: The only way I can explain it is that there was an energy *with* that Light.

Doc: Yeah, yeah, *Divine* Energy.

Susan: You know, like an angel. People mis-use angels and I hate to even use that word, but there was this Divine Light and there was no "being" there...

Doc: Divine Presence, yes...

Susan: There was just this *Energy* that was all-engulfing and unusual. And that's when I knew that we had to do something. Now, he had already written *Power vs. Force*, but he wasn't speaking at all. People would ask him to speak, and he said, "No, I'm not gonna speak." And that's when we decided we better do it—giving lectures and speaking on this.

....

Fran: So, what do you see as your role (Susan) with this Devotional Nonduality community after Doc passes? People look to you, Susan. There's such a love there, a gratitude and appreciation for you.

Susan: You know, I can't really tell you what my role will be. It will happen how it happens. I can't look into the future and say, "Oh, this is what I'd like to happen." All I can say is that I'd like for the work to continue. He has put a whole lifetime into this, and it should continue. As far as it goes, God's spirit will guide me. I really can't say anything more than that. I don't know how it's going to be ... because he isn't going to be here forever. And Dave and I have talked about it quite often. Emotionally, I don't know how I'll be. As far as it goes spiritually, I know I'm fine. But as far as my emotions, I don't know how it will go. Spiritually, I'll be just great. That part's covered! But I don't know how I'm gonna deal with the emotion...

Doc: What happens is that the miraculous takes over. What was not doable before, becomes doable.

Susan: Usually, I know my own self, and I am fine in crisis. I'm terrific. It's afterwards that I'm horrible. So I can go through a crisis just fine. It's after it's all over that I go, "Oh! How did I *do* that?" But you know who you are and how much you can handle.

Doc: God's grace handles it.

....

October 1, 2008

We meet again in his cozy little office. The large dog, Kelsey, and two of the cats have settled in with us.

Doc: Without Susan, I would really be lost...

Susan: Sometimes he just can't track things. He can't track simple sequences when he's really into spiritual spaces.

Doc: That's right, the linear domain.

Susan: The normal person connects this to this to this. *She gestures with her hands, moving from one thing to another in a sequential line.* But he doesn't track it that way. For him, the two things are entirely separate. They look like they should inter-twine, and a normal mind would connect the two things. But when he's in some spiritual states, he can't connect them. He sees each thing in its own box, you could say, in its own dimension.

Fran: Oh. So, I see two things and automatically hook them together. I guess I'm actually projecting a causal link onto them. But he doesn't see that link?

Susan: Yes. *Gesturing with her hands, she identifies three isolated objects in the air.* So, for him, this is separate, this is separate, and this is separate. He doesn't connect them. For example, he doesn't connect the two ideas of: "When it's time for the lecture to start, I need to walk to the podium."

Doc: *Laughing…* Yeah, one eyeball goes this way, and another goes that way! *He gestures two movements in opposite directions.*

Fran: Really?! Even just walking to the podium needs assistance? Why is that?

Susan: Anything with the body, he needs assistance. It's like someone when they are in deep meditation. Things happen all around them, and yet they are unaffected… So, when it requires physical movement to do something, that's when he has the hardest time, because his mind is not with the physical body. Does that make sense? So, in other words, if he's in a really high state, he'll come and look at me in a certain way. And then I have to literally move him to where he needs to be. It happens especially when he's writing about the high states…. When he was writing *I: Reality and Subjectivity*, that book is from such a high state. It was the hardest one for him to write. When he was writing that, he was what I would call "spacey."

Fran: So, the states vary?

Susan: It was different when he was writing *Truth vs. Falsehood,* because he was trying to apply the teachings to the world. So many people think that because you are spiritual, you shouldn't be involved in the world, or there shouldn't be wars and so forth. But there has always been some sort of conflict. When someone is trying to change your peaceful way of life, as in Tibet, of course you want to go back to what it was before they came in to it takeover. I am very saddened by what China did. If there were any way to change it, I would, and to make Tibet its own state. But at this point, how is it possible to change history? There are difficult issues in the world.

Fran: So, you saw him in two different states writing the two different books? In *Truth vs. Falsehood*, there was a tracking of things in the world?

Susan: He had to go back into the world and follow events in order to apply the teachings for people like us, who aren't enlightened mystics and who want to understand the world as it is. Not everybody's in the same place on the Map of Consciousness®. Perhaps everyone wants to try for the higher states, but you have to accept where you are at the time. You can't *force* being enlightened! Some people want to force it. "If I do this or act like this, then I'll be of a high calibration!"

Laughter...

Fran: Now, Susan, was this an issue for you too? In meeting him, did you have to let go of wanting to be enlightened yourself?

Susan: No. It'll happen when it happens—that was my feeling. Why force it? I don't even know what I calibrate at, and I don't care!

Doc: No, she didn't have spiritual ambition. She was not *ambitious* in that way, to "get ahead" spiritually.

Fran: So, there's a difference between devotion and ambition?

Susan: Yes. Devoted without the ambition. Without gain.

Doc: She just got it by propinquity, you see? She entered a field that was compatible with her inner self, but she wasn't trying to get an "A" in it!

Susan: Yes, that's exactly how it was. I wasn't ambitious. I figured he could take me there if he wanted to. I didn't have to "do" anything! I really believe that, one day, I will get to that higher spiritual place, but right now, if we were both there, it wouldn't work!!

Fran: Well, yes, somebody's got to make the espresso and run the place!

Laughter...

Doc: Well, it comes on unexpectedly. There was no warning. It's like a light suddenly comes on. In an instant, you are in that state.

Susan: And he goes into that state even now sometimes. Like when we put on operas in the car, driving back from the cabin. It's like suddenly you're there. The opera is playing, and you're seeing the beautiful scenery as it's going by, and it's almost...

Doc: Magical.

Susan: Yes, magical.

Doc: You're listening to grand opera as you're driving through such beauty and it's...

Susan: Neither one of us says anything. And the body just automatically does what it's doing. I suppose if I needed to snap out of it, like if a deer ran across the road, I would snap out of it. So, no, I've never wanted to be "higher" or "more enlightened." I figure that, eventually, I will be there. In each lifetime, each person needs to be where they are. You can do things toward becoming a better person, like through selfless service. You can do things that raise awareness, in every way and every day. But I don't say, "I'm going to meditate to become enlightened," or try to force it in anyway. There are many paths to enlightenment, not just meditation or deeds.

Doc: Or saying the rosary!

Susan: Oh yes, saying the rosary or spinning the prayer wheel will "make" me enlightened! Chanting every day—that will "make" me enlightened! These are the beliefs.

Fran: So, you're saying there's no cause and effect to spiritual devotion, like: "If I do this, then enlightenment will happen"?

Susan: You can't make it happen. You can't force it, like, "If I sit here long enough, then it will happen!" That's what some people believe. You have to understand that enlightened beings are rare.

Doc: *Talking with Kelsey the dog, who has come over to lay her head in his lap.* Oh come over here, sweetheart. Woof, woof, let me kiss you! Oh, you wanna give me a kiss? Oh you're a sweet dog!

Fran: Susan, were you aware of enlightenment as a spiritual reality before you met Doc?

Susan: Oh yes. Let me think about how to put it. It was always in my being. It's like he would tell me things and be surprised that I wasn't surprised! It's as if I already knew it. He expected me to be surprised at some of these things. It's like an *inner knowing* was already there. It's hard to explain.

....

Fran: When I interview the students of your work, they say, "We want to hear from Susan what it's like in the everyday life."

Doc: *Chuckling.* ... I told you that was going to happen, years ago.

Fran: I guess it's that we're curious.

Doc: Well, it's natural. She's an *inside observer.* It would be that way with, "What's it like to live with Pres. George Bush?" Well, you have to ask his wife, Laura Bush! She's the only one who knows!

Fran: Right. In your case, people perhaps have this fantasy that it's Bliss Central at your house around the clock. What I've seen in coming here is that—along with the extraordinary situation of a mystic in the house!—you have an ordinary home life. It's very tender and loving and you have constant demands with Veritas Publishing, yet the household is also quite ordinary in many ways.

Susan: Yes. The bliss is always present. That is true. It doesn't leave. But then you have to do the other things too. Now, if I had to say one virtue that is needed, I would say "patience." Without that, you'd just run the household as if he weren't here. Things have to be done, but sometimes they are not finished or need to wait so that he can discuss them. Yes, patience is the key, I would say. And sometimes I have lots of it, and sometimes I don't!

Laughter...

Fran: So, Doc, you've said you were aware of an obligation—a contract or a karmic...?

Doc: Responsibility...

Fran: Yes, responsibility to be what you are to the world. And, Susan, would you say that also applies to you?

Susan: Yes, yes it does. There's a contract that I'm supposed to be doing what I'm doing...

Doc: An agreement... an understanding...

Susan: Yes, an agreement and an understanding....

Doc: There is no compulsion about it. So, the understanding was, "If I'm going to be in the canoe, I'll help paddle."

Fran: You came in with a paddle, Susan?

Silence....

Susan: I guess the relationship with us is that he's the teacher. I learn lessons every day, living with him. Some require patience and others do not, and some require understanding. And when he says, "It was an understanding," that is exactly right. It's a complete understanding that we're doing *exactly* what we're supposed to be doing at *this* time, in *this* life. I don't know any other way to put it.

Fran: Susan, was there a point early on when you weren't sure whether you were called to this task, or was your agreement immediate? I mean, it's quite an unusual life!

Susan: Oh, I was very apprehensive. I thought, "Do I really want to get involved in all of this?" Yes, I would definitely say there was some hesitation.

Doc: Well, it was partly a lack of familiarity.

Susan: Yes, part of it. "Unfamiliar," because you think the arm thing is weird! I mean, the teachings themselves are there, and then you add this thing of "I need your arm to ask a question." That was kind of strange. But then you see what happens when you follow the arm and you say, "Oh there's something to this!" So, it's a learning process.

....

Fran: In terms of spiritual teachings, were you raised in a religious family?

Susan: I was raised Presbyterian.

Doc: Her father was a deacon.

Susan: Yes, he was a deacon in the church. We went for about 4 hours of church on Sunday. I think we all had 10-12 years of perfect attendance in Sunday School. We got the pins and everything!

Doc: *Chuckling.* ... Oh, so that's how you get into heaven! Ten years of perfect attendance in Sunday School! And actually, it's staggering when you look at.

Susan: Well, I lived in a small farming community in the Midwest. And when you live in a small place like that, the only social life is through school or church on Sundays. That was just a known fact. You went to church on Sunday. But, I don't know if that made everybody a better person!

Laughter...

Susan: When we were younger, we had strong spiritual ties to certain churches, to structured religion. Now I think people are realizing that the basic teachings are there, good and bad, in all religions. You don't have to be a Catholic, Protestant, or a Buddhist to understand it. They all have the same good and evil.

Doc: Well, misused with the intention for evil, not *intrinsically* evil.

Susan: Right.

Fran: Susan, it's quite a jump to go from a small-town Presbyterian upbringing into these teachings that integrate Hinduism, Buddhism, and all the world's great spiritual traditions. Was there a middle stretch in your life when you investigated non-Christian religions for yourself?

Susan: No, not really… You come to understand that anyone who worships, whether it's a Hindu, Catholic, Buddhist, Muslim… they're all worshipping the same thing, a Higher Spirit than oneself. It's all One.

Fran: And there was a part of you that always knew that, even if you may not have heard it from your small-town Presbyterian minister?

Susan: Yes.

Fran: I mean, I don't imagine that the preacher stood up in the pulpit and said, "We're all worshipping the One Truth!"

Susan: Oh, definitely not.

Fran: But there was a part of you that knew it?

Susan: That's right. Whether from some other lifetime or not, I don't know. But, yes, some part of me knew that all religions strive for the same thing. They just call it different names.

Each one of us has some kind of spiritual insight and, whichever path we follow, we get there. Maybe the Hindu will come back as a Presbyterian, or maybe I'll come back as a Catholic! It doesn't matter. We're all taking our steps and making our path to a Higher Being and a higher spiritual life.

Fran: I find that remarkable, Susan. I was raised Protestant as well, but it was a fundamentalist version. So, it was very difficult for me at first to feel at home with a broader spiritual teaching that said, "All paths lead to the One Truth." I thought Christ was the only way. And karma was also a block for me. I was stuck in right versus wrong.

Susan: I don't understand that. I mean, I understand that you had those steps. But, for me, it was like I already had that knowledge in myself.

Fran: Yes, that's exactly what it sounds like.

Susan: Even though I was raised staunchly, somehow I already had the inner knowledge that it didn't matter what religion you were. I can remember it even as a little girl. Back then, the Protestants weren't supposed to associate with the Catholics. That was pretty staunch! And I had a friend who was in Catechism, and she would tell me the stories about the Catholic religion, and I'd sit and listen for hours. She was learning about all the saints. We rode the bus together and I'd listen to all her stories of the saints!

Fran: And with delight?

Susan: With delight! If my mom had known that, she'd have probably gotten upset! The Catholic stories were fascinating to me.

Fran: You appreciated their devotion.

Doc: Yes, that's her nature.

Susan: I just think that we've divided the whole world up into little sects, but no single one is the only true one.

Doc: And it's interesting how a political philosophy also can become a commitment like a religion. Take communism, for example. It's criticized for invading Tibet. But to the communist mind, the Tibetan monkish community had been brainwashed and lost their freedom. The communists thought they were actually *saving* the Tibetans from a primitive, unenlightened ignorance, brainwashed and kept like prisoners in the monasteries and Buddhist enclaves. The communists came to "liberate" the monks who had been taken as children and systematically restricted from any kind of freedom. The communists had an idealistic intention to "liberate" them from what they saw as "brainwashing and imprisonment." It is similar to the far left today that wants to "liberate" people—they want to "save the country." *Chuckling...* So politics can become religious in that way. I understand the people and don't see them as "wrong" for what they are doing. It is not the path that I would follow. But if I were a died-in-the-wool communist, I'm sure I'd be out there trying to liberate people from being monks!

Laughter...

Fran: So, yes, whether religious or political, people can be legalistic and impositional about their particular dogma?

Susan: Well, when you take away all the ritual—Catholic, Protestant, Jewish, Buddhist, the Mormons—you get down to the fact that they are worshipping God or a Higher Truth.

Doc: It's that people get swept away with over-enthusiasm and narrow-mindedness about their own particular view.

Susan: That's where it goes wrong.

Doc: Yes. Like "born-agains" who become cultish.

Susan: That's the mistake. They should embrace all religions with an open heart and see that we're all trying to get to the same place, no matter what path is chosen.

Fran: And you always knew that?

Susan: Yes. It was always an inner knowing. In high school, my friends were of different religions—Jewish, Catholic, Mormon—so I got to learn a lot about the religions in high school, and we went to each other's services. So, yes, I always felt that, no matter which path you take, you end up at the same place.

Fran: Okay, so when did it dawn on you, Susan, after meeting this guy....

Susan: We met through country-western dance class! It was like *I already knew* him! We didn't have to say much to each other because it's as if we already knew each other. He was just very familiar to me.

Fran: Almost like a recognition?

Susan: Yes, like a recognition. It was a comfortable feeling. Like going *home*. I felt relaxed and comfortable. So, when we talked, it was like we'd known each other for lifetimes.

Doc: *Chuckling...* Because we had!

Susan: Some people *search* for a lifetime. I guess in this lifetime, I was one of the lucky ones.

Fran: And when did it dawn on you that it would be more than meeting a life partner—that it was going to be a life of public teaching—and that you had a role or responsibility in that?

Susan: I think we'd known each other for about two years... When I realized that I would be spending a lifetime doing this teaching, all of a sudden, the Koreans came to us and said, "We want you to come to South Korea to teach." The Koreans were the first ones to recognize the work, the first ones to want the book *Power vs. Force*. Maybe it was similar to their religion, Buddhism. I don't know. That's when it really dawned on me what was happening, as we're sitting there in front of hundreds of people in a foreign country! A strange thing happened there. Dave asked me the Jung question. He came over to me and arm-tested: "Dr. Jung is over 500" and my arm went weak in front of all those people! And he looked at me like, "What's wrong?" And then we realized that, since Jung was dead, he had to ask it with "was"—not "is." And then it was accurate. "Dr. Jung *was* over 500" and that tested true. So, you're there standing in front of hundreds of people and that happens, and you don't know why! You go, "Where's the hole that I can crawl into??!!"

Laughter…

Doc: Freud was 499 and Jung around 520.
Susan: Yes, he said, "I've asked this question a hundred times. I know Jung is over 500!"
Fran: It is quite subtle—from "is" to "was."
Susan: Right, and then we got the correct answer.

….

Doc: You want some espresso?
Fran: No thanks, Doc.

Doc excuses himself to get some espresso.

Fran: Okay, so when the experience of the Light occurred….
Susan: That happened before we went to Korea…
Fran: It woke you up to, "Alright, we're going to be teaching"?
Susan: That's it. We started teaching, and I knew that's what we were supposed to be doing. Don't ask me why the Light happened. I have no idea. I would say I was open to it, but I wasn't looking for it. It just happened. At the time I didn't know why it happened. Now I know. But honestly, if you had told me that it was going to happen, I would have laughed at you! "Okay, Susan, you're going to see this Light, and it's going to change you forever"—Oh sure, right!

Laughter…

Fran: When it actually took place, however, it was undeniable?
Susan: It was nothing of this world at all. It was a holy reverent

feeling. It wasn't scary, like "Oh no what's happening here?" It was almost like a *knowing*, a recognition of a spiritual base. Maybe it was something that was always there. And I hate to say it, but it truly was like a "Guiding Light." That's what it was. And it hasn't happened since then.

Fran: Is it still guiding you?

Susan: I'm sure it is. It went right through my *being*. If you can imagine a Light coming into your heart chakra and then going through your whole body, that's what it was. And it filled the entire room, and I was part of the Light. I was *part* of the Light. And that Light is still *within* me. It's still there. It was almost like a trigger or a switch or whatever. I think Dave had the same kind of experience. It seems to happen to people when they ask, "What is God's will? What am I supposed to do?" I didn't ask those questions, but he did.

Silence…

Susan: It may be that people who hear about this will say, "I want that to happen to me." But you can't force it. It's God who chooses. And you don't know which lifetime it will occur. But when it happens, it changes everything. I wonder if people who enter a convent have such a life-changing experience like that. When they commit their whole life to Christ, I wonder if it's because they had an experience like that. It is a devotion, whether you are a priest, nun, or a regular person.

Fran: Beyond words?

Susan: That's what Dave said when he was writing *I: Reality and Subjectivity*. The hardest thing is to try to put it into words. How do you do it? The verbalization is the hardest thing – What were you feeling at the time? What exactly happened? How did it change you? I mean, it would take me a *whole book* to answer those questions!

….

Now, fourteen years after those dialogues, Susan *has* written a "whole book"! This book begins with her life before she met Doc. Like him, she grew up in the Midwest. Her family lived on a farm near a small town. When they moved to Phoenix, Arizona, she thrived in the culturally diverse atmosphere of a large city. Among other passions, she loved to dance, and that is how she met Doc. It was a lightning attraction. As Doc and Susan mentioned in the dialogue you just read, they recognized each other from other lifetimes. In the chapters that follow after their first meeting, Susan shares about the evolution of their relationship, their life together at home, being on the lecture stage, and traveling on the road. Note: Some of the highlights that you just read in the Dialogue with Doc and Susan will be repeated throughout Susan's narrative. Doc taught that repetition of something, in a slightly different context, helps us to internalize it.

Readers who already respect Dr. Hawkins as a teacher will feel an even deeper appreciation for his uncompromised commitment to do everything he could out of love for God and others. Susan's account of him "behind the scenes" reveals his authenticity as a teacher who remained true to the highest calling of selfless service and total surrender of his life and will. He had no interest in "followers" or pleasing others; there was no "self" that needed anything from others. Susan writes: "A lot of people are one way in public and another way at home, but not Dave. He was the same kind, wise, funny, and loving man, whether he was on stage or at home."

He was, to the very end, a servant of the Lord. In the final section of the book, Susan gives an account of his passing. Over the years, many people have asked her about his physical dying, but it needed to be the right time to share it. As you will see, the experience was both heart-rending and humorous. She closes the book with her reflections about the significance of the body of work that he left for us and how we can honor it by living it. She encourages us to serve exactly as we are, and to "prioritize our soul" amidst the endless distractions of earthly life.

This book is a treasure, unique in the realm of spiritual literature. We see why Dr. Hawkins trusted Susan completely. She expresses herself openly, without artifice; she has a big heart and abundant common sense. Her book is conversational, inviting us inside her life with Doc. One thing is for certain: Without her loving care and collaboration, he would not have been able to write his books and give his lectures. His body of work, which has touched the lives of millions of people, was made possible by the life he shared with Susan.

—Fran Grace, Ph.D., editor

PART ONE:
"CAN I HAVE THIS DANCE...?"

1

MY LIFE BEFORE DOC

I believe that each of us has a destiny and that we will be given the experiences we need to fulfill it—if we choose to see it that way.

Small Town

I grew up near a small town in the Midwest. My family lived a mile and a half outside of town, on a country farm of about 160 acres. My great, great grandfather bought this land from the railroad company for 50 cents an acre. We lived there until I was twelve.

Growing up in this environment gave me a solid foundation in faith and farm life. I was fortunate to be surrounded by people who worked hard and had strong communal values. Running a farm wasn't easy, but my parents did well to provide for their four young children, and they raised us to be respectful of God and other people.

Socially, as far as my personality goes, the small-town life sometimes felt constricting. There were only one thousand people in the entire county, so it was like living in a fishbowl. If you got into trouble, everyone knew about it! If you got a new dress, people knew exactly where it came from and how much you paid for it. There was sometimes a judgmental atmosphere that didn't suit me. I never understood why people would be unkind to each other. As a little girl, these questions were always in the back of mind: Why are they treating this person like that? Why are they picking on this person because of this or that? I would not step in to stop it because, back then, a girl could not do that, but it bothered me when people judged and mistreated others.

My nature has always been free-spirited and fun-loving. To give you an idea of my sense of humor, here is a story. They used to call girls from the Midwest "heifers." One day, I heard a man say this, and I quipped back at him: "I'm hungry. I think I'll go out to the field and eat some grass!"

My mother was the serious type, and she would raise an eyebrow at my humor. She was always telling us, "Now, don't do *that*! What will the neighbors think?" Even decades later, when I was travelling with David to the great cathedrals in Europe, my mother was upset at me for sending her a postcard that said: "I've been to so many cathedrals here. If I'm not holy by the time I get back home, I never will be!" She told me, "Now, Susan, what were you thinking? Don't you know people read that?!" I was being playful, but she didn't get the joke.

As a young girl, whenever I felt stifled, I prayed to God to get me out of the small town. When my father was offered a job in Phoenix and we moved, I felt like that was an answer to my prayer. My early years in the Midwest, however, contributed positively to my development in several areas. In fact, it was there that I learned some of my most significant lessons about life and spirituality.

Early Spiritual Experiences

There's nothing like a tornado to instill faith. I remember one experience, in particular, that was terrifying but also comical (in retrospect!). It was summertime, and my dad had invented a cooler with a garden hose and box fan, which we kept in the window to blow cool air into the house. If you've ever been to an old farmhouse in the Midwest, you know that it's hot and humid in the summertime. The minute you get out of the shower, you feel like you need another one. At nighttime, you throw off the sheets and pray for a breeze. Our only air conditioner was the homemade cooler that my dad made out of a box fan.

One night, we were all asleep. When it started to rain, my dad was lying in bed and thought, *Oh good, maybe it'll get a little cooler.* Then, it started to hail. He lay there for another minute. And then ... dead silence. My mother jumped up and shouted, "I know it's a tornado coming!" She bolted to the other end of the house where my brother and sister were sleeping; they were in their teens and hard to wake up, so she had to yank them out of bed. My father ran to another part of the house to get my other sister and me out of bed. We were the younger ones. He grabbed our hands and flew us down three flights of stairs toward the basement. I say "flew" because we went so fast, my feet never touched the ground. My brother, about sixteen at the time, was at the bottom of the stairs trying to shut the outer door of the basement. It had flown open with the wind, and he was fighting to get it shut so that we wouldn't be swept up into the howling cyclone.

In the meantime, the box fan that my dad had used to create the cooler was spinning in the open window and hurling hailstones across the living room, ruining everything. Just imagine lamp-shades pelted by hail! I laugh about it now, but it was scary when it was happening. My dad finally had to run outside into the lightning storm to grab the fan out of the window so it would stop throwing hail stones into the house. The next day, we sucked up an ocean of water from that carpet.

The storm was ominous. I peered, wide-eyed, out of the basement window. Every time there was lightning, the entire scene lit up and I could see the tornado coming right at us. But, the truth is, I felt a strange peace inside. I remember thinking, *We're gonna be okay. It's gonna jump over the house.* Spiritually, I wasn't afraid because I knew it was going to jump over the house and we wouldn't be hurt. And that's exactly what it did. It bounced a couple of times on the ground and then it flew right over the house.

It was a close call. Our house could have been destroyed. We could have died. It was one of those moments when you know that your life is not your own; in a split second, you could be swept up into a torrential wind. I remember what I felt in that moment. It was an all-pervading peace. *God is with us, and we are protected.* That was my very first spiritual experience.

I had another spiritual experience during childhood that stays with me to this day. It was my first encounter with death. My dad hired a man to live on the farm and help us with the work. He and his wife were just like grandparents to us. She was diabetic. One day, unexpectedly, she went into a coma and died. When my mother looked at the dead body, she was so upset that she didn't allow my younger sister and me to see it. We begged her to let us go and see this woman who was like a grandmother to us, but my mom refused. Finally, when mom wasn't looking, we snuck a peek at the body. The dead woman looked so peaceful and so beautiful. As I stared at her, suddenly a deep peace came over me. Even though I was just a little girl, I knew what had occurred, spiritually. I thought, *All of her trials of being here on Earth are over.* She looked angelic and peaceful. I was never afraid of death after that.

There was spirituality on one hand, and religion on the other. In terms of religion, we were members of the Presbyterian Church, and this gave me a foundation of faith. My father was a deacon in the church. We went for several hours of church every Sunday. I think each of us kids had 10-12 years of perfect attendance in Sunday School. We got the pins and everything! When you live in a small town, church is the main social event. Almost everybody went to church on Sundays. Did that make us better people? Maybe so. But it also felt sterile to me because they didn't believe in beautification of the church. It lacked art and expression. Also, they were sectarian. Those aspects did not fit with my inner knowledge.

You see, from an early age, I knew that it didn't matter what religion you were. Back then, some religions did not mix. For example, Protestants were not supposed to associate with Catholics. That's what I mean by "sectarian." I had a close friend who was Catholic. While she was going through her Catholic Catechism, learning all about the saints, we rode the bus together and I loved listening to her stories about the saints and her religion. If my mother had known I was learning about Catholic saints, she would have been upset. But, for me, I knew that all religions were striving for the same thing, seeking the same Truth and calling it by different names. I didn't hear that from the church we attended. It was an inner knowledge, deep inside of me, maybe from some other lifetime. I was aware that the world was divided up into little sects. It was strange to me that many of them claimed to be the "only" true religion, because I knew that no single religion had a corner on the truth.

Wisdom from the Farm

One valuable lesson I gained from the farm was my love for growing things. Even now, every year, I plant seeds and harvest squash, lettuce, kale, tomatoes, and more. On our small ranch in Arizona, where David lived when I met him, we have an orchard full of fruit trees—pomegranate, pear, peach, apricot, and apple, to name a few. I love seeing things grow, whether it's vegetables, trees, money, or talent! Sometimes the wildlife come and eat up my lettuce. I share this land with bunnies, deer and javelina, and they know where to come for a good meal and that's fine with me. Like the old farmers in the Midwest would say when a crop failed, "We'll just have to replant the seeds and start over."

There's a lot of wisdom that comes from living on the land, and I'm grateful for my years on the farm because of that. David and I both grew up in the Midwest with farm animals and knowing how to grow things. He and I shared a love for animals and gardens. He often said, "We're only responsible for planting the seeds, not the results."

Another wisdom from the farm was this: "You don't have to get even—the Universe will take care of it." That was one of my father's mottoes, and he lived by it. One time, a grain broker took advantage of him. Instead of going after the person who had done the wrong, my father said, "The Universe will take care of it," and then he let it go. Sure enough, that person ended up paying for what he'd done. Years later, when I told my father's motto to David, he said, "That's similar to a Buddhist's view of karma."

Just recently I remembered something else that my father taught me. It saved the day—and gave me a terrific laugh! I had just picked up new baby chicks from the Feed Store, and they were in their little box. We get baby chicks every spring for the Happy Eggery chicken house that Dave built at the ranch. As I was driving down the winding Upper Red Rock Loop Road, suddenly the top of the box flew open, and a baby chick jumped out and ran across my dashboard. Have you ever tried to drive on a curvy road with a chicken running back and forth across your dashboard? I was fretting, *He's going crazy and might hurt himself!* And then I remembered what my dad told me, "It's easy to calm down a chicken—just turn on music." So, I hit the radio button and what came on? The Beach Boys singing, "Let's go surfin' now - everybody's learnin' how - come on a safari with me...!" And, sure enough, the little chick sat right down on the dashboard. When I got home to the ranch, I was able to catch the little chick and put him back into the box, but I didn't shut off the music until he was in there!

You can see by now that folks from the Midwest are down-to-earth and practical. This way of being has served me well in my life with David and our work together. I've never been one of those "spiritual" people to put on fairy airs or walk around in white robes, "holier than thou." To me, the path is pretty simple: Help others whenever possible, and get your hands dirty to grow whatever you can. My mother had a favorite saying that we put on a plaque: "Kissin' wears out, but cookin' don't!" We Midwesterners are known for our common sense, and that's something that Dave and I both appreciated about our upbringing.

Moving to the City

I'm grateful for everything I learned on the farm, but I was thrilled
when we moved to Phoenix! My dad got tired of farming, so
he went back to school for engineering and was offered a job in
Phoenix in the space industry. He couldn't tell us exactly what he
did because it was classified, but we knew it had something to do
with spacecraft blueprints. We found out thirty years later that he
had created many of the things that are flying around in space.

Moving to Phoenix changed our lives dramatically. My whole
family complained about Phoenix because of the hot weather, but
I didn't mind it. I thrived in the bigger schools and blossomed
in the more open-minded and diverse atmosphere of a large city.
Free from the gaze of small-town gossips, I felt like I could finally
breathe and be myself. I had prayed to God to get us out of the
small town. And, so, when we moved to Phoenix, I had the feeling
that God was watching over me. That inner security continues to
the present day.

In high school, I hung out with a social climber crowd. I never
got into drugs or "trouble" per se, but I didn't exactly fit into the
expectations of my family either. For example, at a young age, I
was drawn to beautiful art and music, and I loved watching opera
on television. My dad would say: "Turn that howling off!" And my
mother was not happy with me when I got close with Mormon
or Jewish friends. I enjoyed going to religious services that were
different from what I grew up with. I was committed to seeking
Truth, not following dogmas.

Love of Beauty

When I was seventeen, I followed my heart and went to the Flair
School of Modeling. After finishing their program, I put myself
through school by modeling jewelry and clothes at events and on
runways. It was fun, and I'm told that I was good at it. One time, I
had the surreal experience of wearing an emerald necklace that was

worth more than a house, and they posted guards all around me. In the modeling arena, especially nowadays, a lot of people get caught up in their physical appearance to the point where it is destructive to their bodies and psyches. To me, it was never that way. I just enjoyed the social dimension and aesthetic value of it.

I've always appreciated beauty, in whatever form. It was not the outer image that attracted me but the inner essence of something. Art, for example, expresses something beautiful of the human spirit. I developed a special fondness for the craftsmanship of fine jewelry. When Dave and I were together, he loved getting me jewelry whenever there was a special occasion. He taught that "beauty is a path to God." Even as a young woman, I knew that beauty was an aspect of life to respect and enjoy.

In my twenties and thirties, I worked in various small businesses, galleries and boutiques throughout Arizona. I enjoyed being a steward of beauty, whether it was jewelry, clothing, or art, and seeing the businesses grow. Life was not easy in those early years. There were times when I wasn't sure I would make ends meet, but I was resourceful. Just like David, I've always been a hard worker. At age of five, I hunted down spare change in our family's couch and saved up for my favorite candy! When I started to earn more, I had the joy of sharing it with others. One of my favorite lines is from *Hello Dolly*: "Money is like manure. It's not worth a thing unless it's spread around."

Life Lessons

I learned a lot about life and human nature during this time. I had my share of heartbreaks and hard times, but those were the lessons I had to learn. First, I learned to respect myself. People are disrespectful to those who do not respect themselves.

Second, I learned to respect others enough to listen, rather than point a finger. When there's a conflict, I take responsibility to look at myself and own my part. What did I do to incite this? Could I have handled it better?

Third, life doesn't always seem fair, but give it time. "Sometimes you're the windshield, and sometimes you're the bug. Sometimes you're the bat, and sometimes you're the ball." That is how Winona Judd phrased it in her song. Life can seem unfair, but I've learned to wait for the deeper purpose to reveal itself. Sometimes a door needs to slam in your face so that the next one will open. If someone breaks up with you, that means something better is on the horizon.

Fourth, your mistakes make you wiser in the long run, so why beat yourself up? Life is our greatest teacher—if we learn from our mistakes.

During this time, I continued to expand spiritually even though I was focused on making my way in the world. I met someone at work who invited me to several Hopi ceremonies, including a traditional Hopi wedding, on Second Mesa in Arizona. Looking back, I realize what an honor it was to be invited, especially to the Snake Dance. Now, I am told, white people are no longer invited to the Hopi ceremonies, because they were not respectful of Native ways. David, before I met him, was also invited to the Hopi Second Mesa to attend the Snake Dance. Perhaps we were there together and didn't know it. Our lives were interwoven in ways we were not aware of until later.

Out of respect for the privacy and sacredness of their traditions, I will not go into detail about the Hopi ceremonies that I saw. I will just say that their faith in prayer, and their respect for the earth, made a deep impression on me. These are primal truths that the rest of us have yet to learn. We want to possess and exploit the land. We don't respect it. We need to learn from the Native peoples to care for Mother Earth and have reverence for all of life. It makes me very happy to see that my granddaughter loves snails and all sorts of little creatures. She built a terrarium and is studying their habitat. She is learning that every creature, no matter how small or slimy, plays its part in creation.

I learned from a young age to understand and accept people's belief systems, to see that each of us is working to be a better person in our own way. I never got hung-up with religious differences. I saw that all cultures and all religions have their rituals and beliefs that they hand down to their loved ones. They may look different in their outer forms, but there is a common thread that runs through them all, and that is to teach respect, love, and compassion. When I met David, and I saw his Map of Consciousness® for the first time, I recognized instantly that he had found a way to express these truths in a unique format that could help mankind.

Questions and Answers

Q: Even though your upbringing was strict Presbyterian, have you always been open-minded about diverse religions?
A: I was never a devout religionist, but I was brought up with a Christian foundation and I loved to learn about all the different religions. It was an inner knowing. God does not play favorites. I always felt that, no matter which path we take, we end up at the same place. Each religion has its own rituals and beliefs, which are actually just traditions that are handed down. They each have a different focus. Catholics put priesthood on a pedestal, whereas Hindus want to live a good life and die by the Ganges, etc. Each one of us has some kind of spiritual insight and, whichever path we follow, if we are true seekers, we will be given what we need to find what we are searching for.

Q: What is your advice for spiritual seekers? I ask as a woman in India, on a spiritual path.
A: The teachers are usually men. When I grew up, all the ministers and religious leaders were men. We women are usually the nurturers. We nurture people, children, husbands, and family. So when we step out and say, "I want to follow this spiritual path," then it can be challenging because it goes against the norm and people may not like it. Society keeps trying to put us back in the box, and that's okay, because change takes time. We're beginning to have women priests now, in a lot of different religions, and that is a very difficult

path to follow. But a spiritual path is one that we choose from the heart as well as from the mind, because that's how women operate. So, I would say that it's going to take some time for social changes to emerge, and for society to realize that we do already have spiritual teachers among the women. It's a hard path for women to follow, because it has been set up by men.

Mother Teresa is a great example. I saw where she slept at her convent in Rome, and it was on a cot in a closet-like room with just a light bulb in a socket dangling from the ceiling. She gave up everything and all the amenities that we would consider as important, and she dedicated her life to humanity. If she can do it, we can do it. We can all do something to help humanity.

As a spiritual seeker, do what you can to make it easy on whomever is your teacher. What I mean is: Everyone has problems, but it's not necessarily the teacher who has to solve those problems. It's up to you as individuals to work to solve your problems, and some can be solved through just talking them out loud with a caring person, sponsor, therapist, or someone like that. Emotionality and egotism have no place in the ashram or spiritual group. It's best if you can get to know yourself, understand your inner workings, be aware of your inner psychology, so that you recognize when your ego is taking over. This will help you become a better spiritual student. The ego can sneak in, or your personal issues, and you have to be able to catch that. It means you have to be aware of your subconscious, which is hard to see on your own.

A lot of people have a "spiritual ego" that comes in and takes over, and they're not even aware of it. It's because they want to be recognized for the work that they're doing. They may have some childhood issue there, something that needs attention. In doing spiritual work, we are not here to be recognized. We are here to be of service to each other, and to absorb the teacher's work and to absorb the meaning behind it, and to work toward our spiritual fulfillment by surrendering ourselves. It's hard to be in the student's position, and it's hard to be in the teacher's position. Sometimes we don't like doing what we're asked to do, and we have to do it anyway. That's the hardest part—doing what needs to be done, rather than what *you* want to do!

There are certain things that have to be done in order for everything to run smoothly, and you have to do them. Many times, this means you have to "eat crow." You apologize. When I'm in the wrong, I say, "You're right. I am sorry. That was wrong of me to say or do." I did what I thought was best at the time, but sometimes being a woman, emotionality comes into it for me. The true spiritual aspirant is someone who is willing to do something for the all, and not be patted on the head about it. And that's hard to do.

Q: Can you talk about the role of virtues, given that it is so tempting to shoot for the stars?
A: What is virtue? It is a label that's put on something. Or maybe an idea that people have in their heads about how they're supposed to be. Where I grew up in the Midwest, people held to certain virtues. Some of those virtues were good, and some were not very good. Some of their "virtues" were overly staunch and judgmental.

Sometimes spiritual people want to walk around as if they are covered in white robes, all perfect and full of virtue. They have an idea in their head about how they're supposed to be—pious, moral and so on. They're thinking, "Oh, I'm holy. I'm so virtuous." But, in reality, it's just a persona, so they are fooling themselves.

What matters is what's in the heart, which maybe no one sees but God. Dave taught us to be humble, to be kind and to just be yourself. It's not about acting virtuous or striving for a certain state. People often want to get to the "highest level" that they can possibly get to. That's probably not going to happen any time soon, I'll tell you; there are not very many people in the 500s and higher. People want to be "higher," or they're deluded to think they already are! My advice is simply to be a genuine person, a real person, a kind person.

Q: How do I increase my level?
A: To increase it, you have to look at what you need to improve

in yourself. Sometimes this means letting go of habits and beliefs about yourself that you grew up with. If you're too permissive and too giving as a person, if you let people walk over you, then maybe you need to work on that. I'm not saying to address those people directly, telling them that they're walking over you. Instead, you just stop letting them. You stop the habit from *your* end of things. Distance yourself from whatever does not have integrity. You may notice that you're hanging on to certain people or patterns, and you have to be willing to let them go. You have to realize that the only way to get out of the cycle that's repeating itself is by you letting go of it. I've had to put my foot down on being tolerant to certain people in my life. And Dave did too. Just because they're family, doesn't mean they can treat you any way they want. Dave told me, "If someone asks you to do something and you can't do it, just say, 'No I can't do it.' Don't tell them an excuse or a reason."

2

MEETING DOC

Dave and I met at a country-western dance class. We saw each other from across the dance floor, and it was an instant recognition. I was never one to believe in love-at-first-sight "lightning bolts," but that's what it felt like.

When he sauntered up to me and asked, "Will you be my partner?," I didn't realize it would be for the rest of my life. Those blue eyes pierced right through to my soul, and I couldn't do anything about it. You might say I was hypnotized.

He was a very smooth dancer. Plus, he was wearing his cowboy hat and boots, and there's just something about a man in a cowboy hat! He and I always got a kick out of that country-western song that says, "Save a horse, ride a cowboy." Dave was down-to-earth, and I loved that about him. From that first dance, we moved like we were one. There is the song, "Can I have this dance for the rest of my life?" And it came true.

The Hand of Destiny

There was a big age difference between us, but it didn't matter to me. When it's right, it's right, and you know it in your heart, if you're open to that. Some people close to me said, "Don't do it! There's too much of an age difference!" But I cast their opinions to the wind, because I knew there was something deeper going on.

Just before I met David, I was thinking, *I'd like to get married,* so I wrote down a list of the traits that I wanted in a partner. Can you guess? Age was not on that list. Now that he's gone, I see the reason that we had to have that age difference—I was meant to remain here to carry on the work after he passed. There were hidden meanings in our relationship that I can look back now and see. Sometimes it works like that. We don't see all the answers at first.

Later on, Dave and I did kinesiology and found out that we had been together in 11 other lifetimes. So that's why we recognized each other and why he was so easy to be with. We were just in sync. I think it might be true for anyone, that a strong and special connection with someone is worth waiting for and you'll know when it's right. I was in my 40s, and he was in his 60s. It was as if God came in and said, *This is the one you're supposed to be with!* It takes patience to wait for the right person.

At first, I didn't know the spiritual side of him; I had no idea who he was or what he was, except that we were two souls who had finally found each other. We met at a social event, not a spiritual one, so how could I have known that Dave had a huge spiritual dimension to him?

The hand of destiny is strangely precise. Later on, I found out that Dave and I had had close calls of *almost* meeting several times before we finally did. I'd heard about him many years before I met him. I was at work one day and overheard some doctors talking about a man who had gone through surgery without anesthesia. These doctors marveled at how the man had been able to "go into a trance" while under the knife. After I met David, he told me about his experience of having two surgeries without anesthesia. He was allergic to narcotics and analgesics, so by necessity, he had to find an inner path to transcend pain. These were the extreme experiences he put himself through, just to verify the power of consciousness! He shared his discoveries with all of us. In *Healing and Recovery*, he tells exactly how he went through surgery with no anesthesia. The gist was that he let go of all resistance to the pain, and surrendered his personal will to Divinity. This took him into a state of ecstasy, close to the heart of God. What a remarkable person he was!

The Map of Consciousness®

David did not reveal this spiritual side to me right away. He gave little hints, in his speech and in his mannerisms, and it was a subtlety that slowly progressed. Then, one day, he invited me over to his house to eat dinner with him. To be honest, I knew he wasn't a great cook—his idea of cooking dinner was to throw everything into one pot!—so I ate before I went.

When I walked into his house, I noticed something in the hallway. It was a chalkboard with a chart and numbers written on it. I was intrigued, so I asked him, "What's that?" We stood in the hallway together, looking at it. He said, "That's the Map of Consciousness®." He explained to me that he had created this chart to help people understand themselves and the world. He said, "Each level of consciousness has its own view of life, view of God, view of self, emotion, and process. On a single chart, you see the entire world. It's the level of consciousness that determines how a person sees the world. It shows the pits of despair all the way to the state of enlightenment."

I was stunned by the simplicity and the magnitude of it. As soon as David explained the Map to me, I saw how it could help people. He had worked for decades as a psychiatrist with all kinds of people who were suffering, even cases of extreme mental illness. He knew the importance in psychiatry of giving someone a tool to help them come out of their despair. He created the Map as a tool for learning and inspiration. Just looking at it helps a person to evolve their consciousness.

Seeing the Map was life-changing to me, and I knew it would be life-changing for others. I said to him, "This is really important. Why are you sitting on it? Why don't you write a book?" He said he wasn't sure he wanted to go out into the public, so I said the words I knew he couldn't refuse: "David, this Map would really help people!"

That's the moment when I realized he was much more than a terrific dancer. He had a whole spiritual side to him that was extraordinary. I hadn't been exposed to terms such as "enlightenment," but it's as if the spiritual things he shared with me were already inside my being, and they always had been. When he told me things, he was surprised that I wasn't surprised by them. It's as if I already knew them.

After that moment in the hallway, he didn't hesitate to share spiritual things with me. He started writing his first book about the Map, called *Power vs. Force: The Hidden Determinants of Human Behavior*, which has become very well-known by now, and the rest is history. Little did I know that he'd write many books and we'd spend the next twenty years traveling the world, sharing the Map of Consciousness®.

"Let Me Have Your Arm"

When Dave was teaching me about the Map of Consciousness®, he'd use my arm for the muscle-testing. To be honest, I thought kinesiology was weird at first, because I'd never been exposed to it. He wouldn't state the question out loud. He would simply hold the question in mind and then say to me, "Resist," while he gently pushed down on my extended arm. Muscle-testing, or kinesiology as it's also called, felt strange at first, but my inner knowing assured me it was alright. It made intuitive sense to me that the body would respond to the energy you exposed it to. If an energy is negative, the body goes weak. If positive, the body stays strong. And then, of course, after I had my own experiences with muscle-testing, there were too many confirmations to deny its accuracy. We found we could know the truth about something instantly.

I'll never forget the first time he showed me how to muscle-test. We were at his house and had walked down to the creek, and he said, "Let me have your arm." I said, "What?!" I didn't know what he was after! He said, "I'm going to hold something in mind, and then I'm going to press on your arm." He showed me how to hold out my arm. I didn't know what he asked, but the arm stayed strong. He just looked at me and said, "Okay." I said, "What did you hold in mind?" He said, "I'm not going to tell you." In fact, he never did tell me. My intuition said it was something personal that he wanted to know, about us. I figured that it revealed itself, because we ended up together.

Kinesiology was unfamiliar to me, but then I saw what happened when we followed the arm. At first, I just stuck out my arm for him to push down on, and I didn't care what kind of answer it got. If my arm went down or stayed up, I didn't care. But then as I got more into it, I found that, as we followed the arm, it revealed the truth. I thought, "Oh, there's something to this!" Even if it wasn't the answer I personally might have wanted, the technique would take us to the right spot. I remember one time we used it to track down a missing girl; her case was in the news. I was confused because we were getting that she was in two different states, but that turned out to be the truth of it, because the kidnappers had taken her across state lines. Muscle-testing doesn't always make sense at the time that you do it, but I found it to be very accurate.

Dave and I were an excellent team, but even for us, we discovered that kinesiology did not work for personal questions—for example, about money, situations close to us, or the future. If you have any sort of opinion or preference on something, you can't ask about it and get a correct answer.

Dave did the asking very well. Everyone thinks it's the arm that's most important, but it's not. It's how you make the statement itself. If you do that part well, and if your intention is integrous, then you will likely get accurate answers. When he made the statements, he knew what he was doing. If you have two people, wanting nothing but *the highest good*, and testing something *impersonal*, that's when kinesiology really works. Years later, when we did the research for his book, *Truth versus Falsehood*, I thought my arm was going to fall off because we'd do a hundred calibrations at a time. I never would have guessed, when he showed me kinesiology for the first time, that we'd end up doing it thousands and thousands of times.

Marriage

We knew each other for almost ten years before we got married. He was very loving and attentive. I knew we were destined to be together, but I was apprehensive to take the plunge. I thought, *Do I really want to get involved in all of this?* Something in me knew it was not going to be a typical married life, where you settle down with your mate and enjoy your private life together. I knew it was going to be different from the norm, and that it would demand every fiber of my being. During this waiting period, Dave and I gave ourselves the time we needed. We each had to get some things in order before we were ready to commit to a marriage.

For Dave's part, he was just beginning to come back into the world when I met him. He was still a bit of a recluse, and he knew there was something else he had to do. He had spent several years away from the world, in "a monastery of one," as he called it. He was in states of consciousness that made it impossible for him to function in the world. He lived more in the spiritual realm than the physical one. He said he was often not even in his body. One time he walked past a mirror and wondered, "Who is that?" Then he realized it was his own body. He thought, *Oh my God, it's myself! What a surprise!* He was a recluse during those years. He lived off the grid and hadn't even heard of famous figures like Princess Diana or President Ronald Reagan.

Then he got a call from a facility that needed a psychiatrist. They begged him to come and help. He agreed to serve as their head doctor. It was a correctional facility up on Mingus Mountain for fifty adolescent girls who had serious problems. Most of them had been abused; they'd run away from home and gotten into trouble one way or the other. Their next stop was jail. He was the head doctor there for about ten years. He drove sixty miles round trip in his old Willys truck, several days a week, to go help them. Also, he started to do physician rounds in many of the nursing homes all over this part of Arizona. Suffering people needed him, and that's what pulled him back into the world.

In 1997, I was ready to say "Yes" to joining my life with his. I moved to his little ranch to live with him. Soon after that, we took a train trip to San Francisco, and I accompanied him when he gave a lecture at the UCSF Medical School. It was interesting to see the mixed response. Some people walked out; I think it was too spiritual for them. And others were moved to tears. One woman from Ireland came up to us afterwards, and she asked Dave how she could help her country heal from decades of bombing and violence. He told her that the best way for her people to heal was through the "old ways of nature." She took that to heart. I saw how Dave had the ability to speak into the heart of those who were ready to heal.

We got married in 1999. It was a private ceremony at the ranch.

Spiritual Experiences

After meeting David, I had some spiritual experiences that gave me a glimpse of those higher states that he describes. He told me that things like this would happen to me. It may sound like I'm blowing my own horn, but I'm not, and, in fact, I can't do that.

One day, I was driving home, down Upper Red Rock Loop Road, which is full of switchbacks. I was going slowly, looking at the beauty of Cathedral Rock. All of a sudden, I came around a corner, and it looked like the rocks were breathing. The hillside of rocks was breathing like it was alive. Everything was vibrating in 3-D. It scared me to drive, so I pulled over. I thought, *Am I on drugs? Am I losing my mind?!* Dave told me this would happen to me. He said, "Everything just suddenly dissolves into 3D, like it's right there alive with you." I sat there for a minute and his teachings came back to me. It lasted only a minute or so, but that was the longest minute I'd ever been in. It was like that livingness entered my being, and I was one with everything. The whole world was beautiful. After a while, I was able to regain my composure and drive on down the road.

When I got home, I told him about it. He said, "Yeah, that's what occurs when you are really paying attention to your spiritual side. You'll see things like that." I worried, *Is something wrong with my eyesight or my mind?* But he set my mind at ease and said, "That's one of the things that will happen to you—all of a sudden nature shines forth in its beauty so that every leaf, every twig is shimmering in its aliveness." He had explained this to me before I had the experience, but when it actually happened, I felt a bit unhinged because it was so vivid.

I'd been given a glimpse of the beauty of God's Creation, and then it was gone. Since then, I have learned that, if I focus, this state comes on. I have to be by myself, quiet, and slow everything down. I sit there and, if I look at something in that quiet way, suddenly it turns into 3D. We can all do this, because it's our Higher Self, where we are one with life. We bring on that power of the inner Self and the beauty that God has provided us with nature. When you see people in that state, they are "out of it" and they can't contain their ecstasy, so they might be weeping. I understand where they're coming from. You cannot imitate it or force it. It just happens. I wish everyone could experience it. It's a beautiful state to be in—one with God and Creation and everything around you.

Questions and Answers

Q: Thank you for your work. You're the one who started all of this.
A: I didn't do it. Dave had the knowledge, and I just said, "You've got to share this." That's where I was coming from. I thought that the world should have the knowledge. Someone else (before I came along) had told him not to share it. My role was to say, "You can't sit on this! It will help mankind because it explains why people suffer so much and the way out of it."

Q: Before you met Doc, did you know about mystics or enlightened beings?
A: No, I had never been around people like Dave. He was one of a kind. I don't know if there has ever been another person like him

here on planet Earth. Eventually, it just seemed like a natural thing to me for him to be that way. Had I been hoping to be around someone enlightened? No, that was not my goal. It wasn't even in my mind at all. Did I want to take part in all of this? Not really! I was hesitant because I knew it would require everything of me. Did I think it would turn into this? Not really. It all just happened of its own accord, and I think people gravitate to the energy of the teachings, because it reverberates in our souls. I think it is the energy that draws people into the teachings, because they can feel it comes from the heart.

When Dave talked, it came from the heart. He could see right inside a person and knew what to say to them. I saw him do this at the *satsangs*, when people came up to ask him a question. Sometimes his response was kind and sweet, and other times you got the Zen whack, because you needed it.

That was in his public teaching role, when students were asking him questions. It was different in our personal relationship. David never told me what to do. He let me be myself—completely. In his private life, with all the people around him, he let people be what they were. He didn't give advice because he didn't want to take on the karma of others.

Q: How did your inner life shift after you met Doc?
A: It wasn't really a shift; it was the opening of a door. I was busy with family and work and then suddenly Dave came into my life. And when you have a partner, you try to fit in with their habits, their lifestyle, their destiny. It was a bit of a learning process. He seemed to know that's what he wanted, and that we were meant for each other. How did it open my inner life? My spiritual life was always there, it just wasn't opened up. I hadn't found someone to share in the spiritual part of me. Who better to open up to? I'd say something to David, and he'd go, "That's right." Or I'd say, "Why would this happen? Why would they feel that way?" And he'd explain it in a way that hit the nail on the head. It was coming from the spiritual part of him. And he would make funny little jokes all

the time. We had intense spiritual discussions, but we laughed a lot too. I can't put some of his jokes in this book because some people might get offended; he was not a prude! And I, too, sometimes came up with a good joke that made him laugh. Just before he passed, he told me, "Now, honey, I want you to get married again if that would make you happy." I said, "Oh no, I don't want to do that. Husbands are too hard to train!" We had some good laughs, even at the end.

Q: What was it like to be so close to Doc for long periods of time?
A: Just like being with your own self. Where I began and he left off, there was no difference. We could be together, whether we were together physically or not. It was like that from the first time we met, and it's still that way, now that he's gone. I never thought of my life with him as being special when he was here. It was just the way it was. Now that I look back, I can see how much he did for so many people, how he changed so many lives, how they hung on his every word. Can we ever duplicate that? No. We were lucky to have him with us as long as we did. But, it was also a lot of pressure on me. One time, Dave found me standing in the kitchen in the middle of the night. He led me back to bed. He told me, "Susan, you were sleepwalking." I didn't even know it! When you do that, it means you're under a lot of stress. Would I choose any differently? Absolutely not. Every path comes with its challenges. I'm grateful for all that I've experienced because of David. I like this line by Willie Nelson: "Heaven is closed, and hell's overcrowded. I think I'll just stay where I am!"

3

BEGINNING OF THE WORK

When I married Dave, I knew it was going to be my life's work to assist him in sharing himself with the world. I wasn't sure how it would happen, but I knew the work would go worldwide and help a lot of people. Now here we are, twenty-three years later, and all his books are in multiple foreign translations. I hear daily from people whose lives are changed. In the virtual gatherings we give, there are participants from many continents. It's as if a Light that started in one small corner, eventually spread everywhere.

The Light

In 1998, I had a life-changing spiritual experience that convinced me it was time to start our work. It was about four in the morning. We were lying in bed, and Dave was asleep. Suddenly, I saw a Light in the corner of the room. It was incredibly bright. I watched it grow bigger and bigger until it filled the entire room. It was so bright you could hardly look at it, and if you closed your eyes, you still saw it. This brilliant Light had an Energy in it that felt angelic. It filled the room. Then, without warning, the Light went into me. It changed me. I was not the same afterward.

When David woke up, I told him about it. He said, "It was life-changing." I said, "Okay, I know that! But what was it?!" He said, "Divine Light." He told me that the same Divine Light happened to Bill Wilson when the room lit up with the Presence, and It transformed him.

It was the most unusual experience I have ever had. After that, I knew we had to start the work. The Energy of that Light was all-engulfing, and it went into me. It transmitted the knowledge that we had to start giving lectures and teaching in public.

Unexpected Visitors

Our public teaching started in a surprising way.

When Dave published *Power vs. Force* in 1995, he took a second mortgage out on the house to self-publish the book. He knew that the publishing companies were not ready for it. At first, the boxes of books just sat in a storage shed. He was not one to publicize or market himself. He sent the book to be reviewed in the *Brain-Mind Bulletin* and a few journals in psychology, but other than that, he did not promote the book. He always lived by the principle of "attraction, not promotion" and said, "The book will spread by word of mouth." He had no interest in promotionalism, marketing, or getting "followers."

The first people to show a strong spiritual interest came from Asia. This was quite unexpected! Dave and I were sitting at home one day, and there was a knock on the door. It was a delegation of important people from South Korea who had come to invite him to speak there. The delegation included General Chang Kyeong Seok and Dr. J. H. Moon, a Buddhist teacher who had been trained for many years in India by His Holiness the 14th Dalai Lama. She led an ashram in Seoul. They came because they had read *Power vs. Force,* which had been translated into the Korean language in 1997, by a meditation teacher living here in Sedona who happened to be from South Korea. This was a synchronicity that wouldn't have occurred except by Divine will.

These visitors recognized that David was an enlightened being, and they were determined to get us to South Korea. Frankly, we were dumbfounded that they had come clear across the world, just to extend a personal invitation to visit their country. Dave didn't want to travel that far, but they insisted that our visit was crucial. Intuitively, we knew we had a certain karmic commitment to the Koreans. So, before we even did lectures in Arizona, we went to Korea two times, in 1999 and again in 2000. Over the years, Dr. Moon brought many groups of people from Korea to attend our lectures and meet with us. They attended his last lecture in 2011 and his funeral in 2012.

Teaching in South Korea

When we went to South Korea in 1999, it was our first major teaching trip. It turned out to be wonderful, but the start of it was a nightmare. You have to understand that this was not an easy undertaking for Dave, in his seventies, and he'd also broken one of his big toes before we left home. He is a physician, and he blew it off: "Oh, I'll just tape it to the other toe. But I won't be able to stand on it very long." This meant we had to get him a wheelchair everywhere because he couldn't walk long distances.

Our office staff mistakenly booked us on the flight to San Francisco, *a day late!*, so then we missed our flight to Seoul. There we were, standing with our luggage, deserted, at the San Francisco airport at 2 a.m., having missed our flight to Korea! We walked a while in the cold nighttime wind, and finally we were able to hail a taxi to get into a hotel for the night and re-book ourselves on a flight to Korea the next day. It was quite an ordeal. We got hold of Dr. Moon to tell her that we were not going to arrive in time for our first lecture, which was supposed to be at a university. We felt very badly about that, but there was nothing we could do. Later, when we did the arm, we found out that missing that plane was by Divine Ordinance. Sometimes bad things happen like that, and then you find out it was in order to protect you. It was disappointing and unpleasant to go through the inconvenience, but there was a reason for it.

When we finally got to the airport in Seoul, we had another snafu. The armed guards didn't want to let us through Customs, even though we had an official letter from Dr. Moon stating we were invited to teach there. Police and military were everywhere. They gave us a hard time about our luggage, but they finally let us through and, then, there was no one to greet us! The "welcome committee" from Dr. Moon's ashram had gone to the other airport in Seoul, and so we were on our own to find a taxi driver who could speak English. By this time, we were exhausted and just wanted to get to our hotel. We gave the driver a piece of paper with the name of the hotel written on it, but there was a mix-up in the lettering, so we ended up at the wrong hotel! He backtracked and found our right hotel. I can't describe how relieved I felt finally to arrive at our hotel. It was a beautiful place. Dr. Moon and all the people were there to greet us. From then on, everything was wonderful—almost magical. Getting there was a struggle, but it was worth it. I think that's true about many things in life. If you can persist through the initial difficulties, beauty awaits.

We loved being in South Korea. Our hosts were very hospitable and gracious to us. Dave appreciated how the people of Asia bow to the Divinity within each person.

He gave several lectures, and we did workshops on kinesiology to about 40-50 people. He wanted to demonstrate the basic principles of *Power vs. Force*. In one of the demonstrations, Dr. Moon brought out two bags of greens, one organic and the other with pesticides. Dave held them up, one at a time, and asked the group to hold in mind each bag, one at a time, and do the muscle-test. Everyone went weak with the greens that had pesticide. The fact that positive or negative energy has an instant effect was shocking to the people, but they seemed to "get" it.

On the last day, something extraordinary happened. Dave was speaking at the front of the room, and the whole audience was looking at him. Because of where I sat, I could see out of the windows at the back. I saw a gold light outside and then a rainbow came up. I said to Dr. Moon: "There's a rainbow outside," and everybody ran to the windows. The whole street had turned golden with this gorgeous rainbow.

Koreans believe that rainbows are very special. When they see a rainbow, it's a sign. So that rainbow, on our last day there, was meaningful for all of us. It was absolutely beautiful outside. There was gold—the kind of gold cast that you see sometimes after a rain passes and the sun comes out and turns the light into gold. And then the rainbow came up. They told us that rainbows are very rare there, and in fact, the newspaper had an article on it the next day. A number of other extraordinary things happened while we were there. The people were very open and came with the hope of healing, which occurred spontaneously.

One of Dave's favorite stories to tell from Korea is about Diet Pepsi. Along with espresso, Diet Pepsi is what he lived on. So, at one point during his lecture, he said, "I need a Diet Pepsi," and almost every person in the room got up and left to go find him a Diet Pepsi! Pepsi is not easy to find in Seoul. They had to hunt all around the city and finally found some in a warehouse and brought it to us. Dave never forgot that! It shows the devotion of the people.

We felt honored to be there. The people were steeped in a spiritual foundation, so they recognized the significance of David's work, and also his energy. I think being there affected his energy. Dave loved the people and sharing himself, but it was also hard on him. He was going through a state in which his body was aching all over. When you go up in spiritual knowledge, this can happen. He said that when Divine energy increases like that, it's similar to high voltage. If you plug something of too-high voltage into a circuit that's not wired for it, it fries. Dave was going through something like that. He was aching all over; it was very painful for him. His only relief was to lie down.

One day, we were taking a break from the teaching sessions, and he was lying down in the hotel room. I opened a drawer in our hotel room and found a book about the Buddha. I guess they have those books in hotel rooms in Korea, just like there is a Bible in hotel rooms in the U.S. I was reading through that book, and I noticed that when Buddha became enlightened, it said that his bones ached. I said, "David! I got the answer! This is why you're feeling all that pain!" I read the verse to him, and he said, "That's it. Thank you for reading that." It made him feel better just to understand why he was having all these pains and aches. When we left the hotel, I asked if I could have the book, and they gave it to me. I read the whole book.

In 2000, we went to South Korea again. That's when they bestowed on him the title, "Tae Ryeong Seon Kak Tosa" (Teacher of Enlightenment). "Tae Ryeong" means a huge mountain, so the title was saying that he was a "spiritual mountain," a truly great teacher. Dr. Moon and the Koreans were determined to have us come a third time, but it did not work out that way.

We were scheduled to go for the third visit in September 2001. A few days before we were supposed to leave, I told Dave, "I have this funny feeling that we shouldn't go. There's just something about this trip—we can't go." We talked about it for a day or so, and we decided it was best not to go. Dave said, "I have the same feeling—we can't go." And, so, we called and talked to Dr. Moon. She was very, very, very insistent that we go to Korea. Finally, Dave said, "*I cannot leave at this time. I don't know why, but we have to be here.*" He put it firmly, so she had to accept that we were not going to come. Of course, two days later was the infamous 9-11 terrorist attack on the World Trade Center in New York City. And then we knew why we weren't supposed to go! We would have been stuck in Korea with all those backlogs of flights. It would have been very hard on us physically, and also, we had other engagements that we had to do.

When you look back on such moments, you can see that a Higher Power is guiding you, so it's good to pay attention to that gut feeling. Now, I'm not saying it's always right, but in this case, it was right. It's that still small voice that's inside of you that says you shouldn't do something, or you should just be quiet and not say something. The Higher Power comes through and protects you. It's your intuition, that little inner voice, that says, "Don't go there." We were thankful that we decided not to go. It was a very turbulent time in the world.

The Work Takes Off

When Dave wrote his first book, *Power vs. Force*, I knew it was just the beginning. Even though he said, "I only want to write two more books," I knew it would be more ... and now there are twelve books and counting. In 2001, we published his book, *Eye of the I: From Which Nothing is Hidden*, and in 2003, *I: Reality and Subjectivity*. He referred to these first three books as a "trilogy." They are the foundation of his teachings.

The work took off in 2001-2002. There was no choice but to go with it, even though it was a huge learning curve. Here's how it happened.

One day the phone rang, and a man said, "My name is Wayne Dyer. I'd like to speak with David Hawkins." I handed the phone to Dave. Wayne told him, "Hay House is a big publishing company and they are interested in your book. You can become famous." Dave said, "No thanks. I want the book to go by word of mouth." Dave was never interested in fame or money. He just wanted to help mankind.

Unbeknownst to us, Wayne Dyer was a very popular author and speaker in the spheres of self-help and spirituality. He was on national television and a regular in the major public speaking circuits. Someone had given him a copy of *Power vs. Force*. He said it was the most important book he'd ever read.

When we tested the question with kinesiology, the arm said it was for the highest good to sign a contract with Hay House, allowing them to publish a version of *Power vs. Force* while keeping our right to continue publishing our Veritas edition. (David founded Veritas Publishing in order to publish his teachings.) Wayne began mentioning *Power vs. Force* in his lectures. That was twenty years ago. By now, I think *Power vs Force* has reached over a million people. People were thirsty for spiritual wisdom. David had all that realized knowledge in him, and it was just a matter of how the Universe was going to present the means to share it.

The first time we ever actually saw Wayne in person, it was a few years later. We were in California doing a lecture. We had gone to our hotel to rest and freshen up before we had to go back for the second half of the event. Dave was lying down, but he couldn't rest because of a constant thumping noise outside the door. Someone was running up and down the hallway. Dave was annoyed and said, "What kind of a person would be running up and down the hall?" So, I peeked out to see who it was. It was Wayne Dyer! When he was traveling, he had the routine of running up and down the hotel hallway for exercise.

The Lectures Begin

After we got back from Korea, I asked David, "Why don't we do a lecture here in Sedona?" We looked around and found the Creative Life Center in Sedona, so we rented it. He not only wanted to give an all-day lecture. He also wanted to feed lunch to everyone who attended.

That first seminar, in January 2002, we only had about fifty people, but for the second one, there were over a hundred. And by the third or fourth one, the room was filled, and we had to start turning people down. It became a huge task to feed lunch and snacks to everyone. A helper and I would take the truck to Costco, an hour away, to get the food and drinks for everyone. We looked like Mutt and Jeff with that huge truck full of stuff from Costco tied on the back!

Dave was planning only to do the monthly seminars for one year—twelve lectures. In the 2002 series, he covered the topics he felt were most important. But people wanted more, and so we did more... and more... for another ten years. I made sure that we video-recorded every one of his lectures. For the second year of lectures, we changed to a different venue, so that we'd have more space for people. It was at a local hotel.

I told Dave, "We're not feeding them lunch this time," but he said, "I think we should feed them." And, so, we did. In addition to our seminar people, we ended up feeding quite a few hotel guests who sauntered through our lunch line and helped themselves!

There was no way to tell who was in our seminar and who wasn't. And some of the people literally stuffed their pockets with cookies! It was fascinating to watch the grasping. So, we decided that it wasn't going to work to be that free-flowing and to feed everyone.

We had to be realistic; some people did not respect the offering. This was one of the hard lessons to learn in dealing with the public. Even when you are offering something precious, and working very hard to do it, some people will not respect the gift or the effort. They will try to grab it for themselves. We developed a system of registration and wristbands. And even with that, we had to deal with people who invented ways to sneak in by re-using a wristband. I was shocked by the attitude of some of the people who called themselves "spiritual."

I don't think most people understood the enormous effort that David made to prepare and give these lectures. He made it look so easy, but it was hard for him to function in the world and do everything he was doing for people. When he spoke about higher states, he sometimes would go into those states and then he wasn't able to speak or move. Those states incapacitated him. He had to learn how to speak about the topics and still stand.

At one of our early lectures, in February 2003, Dave walked down the aisle and I could tell he was in that high state. I started to weep, because it seemed like he was going to leave his body, right in the middle of the lecture. The audience was getting nervous. It was bizarre. We got through that day, but Dave and I had to live with the fact that we didn't always know when those higher states might come in and take him over. He needed someone to watch out for him and care for him, and that person was me.

I knew Dave's message was getting out into the world when people started to show up, unannounced, at our house and demand to see him. One time I will never forget. It was a Sunday afternoon, and we were enjoying a quiet day at home, which was rare. There was a loud knock on the door. I was cooking, so I told Dave, "There's someone at the door." He opened it, and this guy said, "Hi! I wanna talk to Dr. Hawkins!" Dave said,

"Well, he's not here." The guy said, "But you look like him."
Dave said, "Well, I'm *not* him!" and he shut the door in the guy's
face! It was a good lesson for me. This was the kind of thing
that David would tolerate up to a certain degree and then that
was enough. The guy had walked down our driveway, into our
private space on a Sunday afternoon, and he thought he was en-
titled to have a personal visit. Dave shut the door in his face. He
said it isn't bad manners to do that if you need to. Just because
somebody wants something, doesn't mean you have to give it.

Questions and Answers

Q: You met Doc after he was in seclusion for many years. As far
as you understand, when he came out of that seclusion, did he
have to acquire an ego or personality in order to function again
with the rest of the world?

A: No, not exactly. He came out of seclusion and realized that he
had more work to do, and the only way he could do it was to be
in the world. He had to rejoin the world in order to do the work
he was supposed to do in his later years. He felt a responsibility to
mankind. That's the best way I can describe it.

I think we have to try to see what this was like for him. Who
wants to come back into the world from such a wonderful place?
But he did. He said that in order to do what he had to do for mankind, which is this body of work that he left us, he had to come
back in the world to do it. There were times he didn't want to come
back into the world, and there were times he didn't want to stay
here. But he did—for us.

When he was taken into a high space, he would just get quiet
and contemplate. He learned how to function in the world enough
to give us this body of work, while still having that higher state in
the background. So that's why he says that contemplation is better than meditation, because it allows you to be in the world. For
people starting out, I think meditation is good. You learn mental discipline and how to focus, how not to get caught in all the

distractions. But David recommended contemplation, where you carry your spiritual awareness with you at all times, in the background, while you are going through your day.

Q: Are there any aspects of what he taught that seem to be frequently misunderstood?

A: The skeptic looks for something wrong, and they've done it to Dave just like they do it to anyone. It's just what the skeptic is. So, yes, there are people out there who like to counter everything that we've done. Dave knew that he was sticking his neck out there to write about the spiritual part of life. I think that's why he wouldn't go public until he had me there to help.

A really old friend of Dave's called one day from Michigan. I answered the phone, and he said, "I just called to talk to Doc. I do that once in a while, because he helped me get sober." I told him we were married. He said, "I knew something had happened, because he would not have gone public unless someone was there with him." He had been following Dave since the early days when he was speaking to recovery groups on the East coast. He said, "I knew something had changed in his life, because now he's talking in public and teaching his work." He was a good friend of Dave's, and now mine. He came out several times to hear the lectures in Sedona.

There are always going to be skeptics, but Dave wasn't bothered by critics. There are so many more, countless people that have had their lives changed by his work. One time after Dave had passed, I went to the Buddha Relics event here in Sedona, and people came up to me and gave me their testimony of how Dave's work got them sober. They were all men. I thought, *Dave, are you here? Can you see this?* Each man came up and told me their testimony of how they quit drugs, how they got sober, how they turned their life around. By the time it ended, there were about 20 men around me. They were all telling me something that Doc had done for them. One of them was a heroin addict who overcame that addiction after he heard Doc. That is a hard addiction to kick, but he is now a functioning young man. I'm just amazed. The Lord works in mysterious ways. And He works through *us* in mysterious ways. Each one of us needs to learn that we are the light that everyone sees.

Q: Do you know of any student of Dr. Hawkins, who, by following his teaching, actually became enlightened?
A: No, I do not. And if they are, how would I know? An enlightened being wouldn't email me to let me know! They wouldn't say anything about it. An enlightened being doesn't run around telling everyone they're enlightened. Dave would never say, "I'm an enlightened being." He just shared the experiences he had. That's the difference. And most enlightened beings are not here among us in society. They are up on a mountain or somewhere like that, changing the world through the inner Self. They're not here. And that's why Dave is such a unique teacher because he was in that state and also was able to speak and write about it at the same time. Swami ji Chidatmananda, our friend and student in India, says it is a huge blessing to have someone like Dave, from the West, understand the Eastern beliefs and write them in their essence. He told me that when he first read Doc's books, he knew that Doc was a true teacher like the sages of India. But Dave would never tell you that he was an enlightened being.

Q: You sacrificed a lot of your own personal life in order to help him with his work.
A: I don't think of it as a sacrifice. It's more of a calling. Just like you have your calling. It is a calling, a destiny, a responsibility to mankind. Dave and I did it together. We had a great time together. The work with him, being with him, learning from him, even doing all the logistics that he needed—that wasn't anything hard. The hardest thing is dealing with people's personalities and egos. People have their own agendas, and they can't see that it comes from their ego; they are unconscious of their ego motives. Dave taught me how to deal with that, and so I do my best to follow the

advice he gave me. He warned me about what was going to happen. For example, we get requests from people who want to take his work and use it in their own way. They say, "All I want to do is help." They don't see that it's actually their own ego that wants to print the Map of Consciousness® on their website or book or whatever. They're interested in associating with Dave in order to further their own personal gain of money, reputation, etc. And also, people mis-use kinesiology to test financial investments and other questions for personal gain. You can't get correct answers for such questions. And if anyone charges you to do kinesiology, it's a scam!

The fact is that David had an important body of work to share with the world, but he needed help to get it done and to ensure its purity. He didn't have an ashram to help him, so God gave him me! I was just one of his followers, and I lived with him.

Q: What did you notice when he was deep into his writing? Did he disappear out the back door and not show up for days?
A: It wasn't like that. When he was doing heavy writing, he'd get up at three in the morning and he would write until six, when I got up at six. And then he'd go back to bed for a while. He kept the little tape recorder by the bed, and he would say a sentence into it, which came to him during the night, and then he'd write about it. A lot of his thoughts came at night. Sometimes the tape in his recorder would snag (he used the old tape cassette recorders), and that was upsetting, but mechanical obstacles are just one of the things you deal with in life.

Q: Living with a spiritual master is the greatest gift of God and the rarest. You are a blessed soul to be with such a master. Was it his will or your choice?
A: He never presented anything in black and white, as his demand or will. It was never done that way. It was always done like this: I would take a problem to him, or I would take something that I was working on to him. He would listen. And then he would tell me

how he thought he would answer it, which was, of course, the best way. But it was never a commandment. I saw it not as a personal blessing, but really more like a duty, to help him produce the work. I think we both saw it as a service we made to humanity. I never put myself in that position where I was "blessed," because that brings up the ego in people when they do that. And so, I never looked at it like that.

We met each other at country-western dance class. I knew him as a person, first, not as a teacher. It was not until I saw the Map of Consciousness® in the hallway on a blackboard that I realized that this man had a spiritual side to him that was very unusual. He told me that he had done a lot of things with the Course of Miracles, and we did the Course of Miracles workbook together. And that helped. I never looked at it as a personal "blessing." I looked at it as more of a life commitment to the work, and that's what it has turned out to be.

Dave and I are doing our best to help mankind, but this isn't about Dave or me. It has never been about us; it's about something greater. We all complain about how the world is. If you inspire one person to change for the better, then that helps the people around them. Dave taught me that the most important thing is the inner focus: change yourself, and you change the world. If I could say one thing to you about this—just take the time to be kind.

PART II:
LIVING WITH DOC

4

DOC AS A HUSBAND

Dave was not only my teacher. He was also my husband and my companion in everyday life. I'd like to share with you a few of the characteristics that made David a wonderful partner. These are qualities that we can all strive for in our family life, no matter whom we live with.

Yes, David was an advanced spiritual being, but we still had all the ordinary things to take care of, just like you—taxes, litter boxes, laundry, and so on! No one "walked on water" at our house. He was a unique person, with a gift for mankind, and I did my best to create an environment that supported his destiny. We saw our work together as the agreement we made before we came into this lifetime.

Playfulness and Humor

One of my favorite things about living with Dave was his infectious sense of humor. I couldn't *not* laugh whenever he was laughing. If I was having a bad day, he would tell me something funny just so I'd start laughing. His humor would carry me through *anything*. This was true even during his last days. And at one point, when my two friends and I thought he was dying, he suddenly popped up from the hospice bed and asked, "Who died? Did I know him?!" We all broke out with laughter, which is exactly what we needed.

Here's another funny story that makes me laugh every time I remember it. One time, pretty soon after I moved in with Dave, he was getting up at 5:30 or so to drive over the hill to the girls' correctional facility on Mingus Mountain, where he was working as the chief psychiatrist. He always drank espresso first thing in the morning. When he had to get up early, he'd set his cup on the counter next to the refrigerator. Well, one morning, he got up, and he saw something furry in his cup and nearly flung the cup out of his hand! A furry refrigerator magnet for kitties had fallen into his cup, and in the dark, it looked like a mouse swimming in his espresso! We laughed so hard about that.

Dave was a lot of fun to live with because he was always coming up with corny little jokes. One of the jokes he told was: "What do you get when you send money to Yemen?" Yemen-aid! It's so corny you just have to laugh. So, humor will get you through a lot. It is important to remember, especially in the stress of everyday life, to have a sense of humor, and especially to laugh at your own mistakes. Life isn't such a heavy load to bear if you can laugh at yourself. Whenever I would launch into how bad everything was, Dave would put his fingers in his ears and make a funny face and sing, "La-la-la-la-la-la..." He was basically saying, "I don't need to hear that," and he did it in such a playful, funny way that I had to laugh. He had a gentle, fun way to reel me in if I went off on a negative tangent.

Before I met him, Dave did an interview with the celebrity Shirley Maclaine, and she said, "When I interviewed the Dalai Lama, he did the same thing you're doing—laughing and laughing." I've heard that the Dalai Lama, when he gives a presentation, says something funny and then starts laughing. That's what Dave did all the time. He said it's because, at that high level of consciousness, the mundane is funny. Even if we're not at a high level, we can still see the truth of that. We look back at something in our past, which was maybe rough to go through, but we have a good laugh and say, "What was I thinking?!"

Dave believed in laughter and its power to heal. He was a physician and he had studied the effect of laughter on health. He said that laughter was the best medicine. He laughed at himself, which then made me laugh too. Who laughs at their own jokes? He sure did! Laughing at yourself gets you out of your ego, so you don't take things so seriously. If you're laughing, that means you're not stuck in some hang-up over something. People are so serious about everything. Look at the road rage people get into, even pulling a gun out. "Just give 'em the finger," is what Dave would say—and he did a time or two!

I remember one time, Dave and I were driving up to our cabin in the woods, and we were behind a big pickup truck pulling a large metal trailer that was going very slowly. It's only a two-lane highway, and there are very few places where you can safely pass a slow-moving vehicle. Every time I got on a flat area where I could pass him, the guy would gun it so that I couldn't get around him, and then he'd slow down again, so I'd be stuck behind him for many more miles. This happened several times. Dave couldn't believe how rude the guy was. "He is not a courteous driver!" Finally, we hit another flat area where I could pass, so I stepped on the gas till we got up to almost 90 mph to get around the guy. As we passed by him, Dave rolled down the window, stuck his right hand out and his middle finger went up! I said, "Thank you! I didn't want to have to do that myself!" I got a kick out of Dave, this old man flipping off someone who was not a considerate driver. It made my day. I loved being with him because he was free to be himself and he took me along with him.

He was natural in how he expressed himself, and he wasn't afraid to play like a clown. One time, he came out on stage at a huge lecture event, waving a rubber chicken in the air and making a wild face as he pretended the chicken was going to bite his head off. The whole audience lit up laughing, which of course is why he did it. He loved making other people laugh because it lifted them out of their ego to a higher plane. He could make a hundred different faces, and you laughed at each one. When he did his imitation of the octopus or the camel on stage, people roared with laughter.

When he and I were out in public, he wasn't afraid to dance. If there was music playing, he would touch my arm and say, "C'mon, Suzie, let's dance," and he'd twirl me around right there. He was a good dancer, very smooth. Dancing was special throughout our whole marriage. We danced anywhere and everywhere, in parking lots, restaurants, grocery stores and doctors' offices.

One time we were at Snowmass, Colorado, where there is a famous Benedictine monastery, and the monks had invited Dave to lecture. We were just walking around the town and looking for a place to eat. We heard this little country-western band, so we started dancing. All of a sudden, we heard clapping! We turned around and saw an entire restaurant patio full of dinner guests who were waving, clapping, and cheering us on. The same thing happened in London. We had gone there to lecture, and we ended up dancing in a little steakhouse that was playing country-western music. Everybody gave us a huge clap. We even danced in the eye doctor's office in Phoenix when we had to go there for Dave's eye treatments. It wasn't a happy occasion, but we made it happy just by dancing to the music.

To be honest with you, I sometimes felt a little sheepish to dance in public. The frozen food aisle—really?! I'd say, "Oh no..." And Dave would say, "Ah, c'mon, honey bunch..." Of course, he was irresistible. He enjoyed the fun side of life as well as the serious side of life. It was a lesson to me that not everything is serious. You can be playful at times when you least expect it. Playfulness and humor are the way to go through life and enjoy it.

Wherever we were, sometimes it was just out of the blue, it was fun to be with Dave because his "little boy" would come out and play. That's what I called it, "his little boy," that is, his playful side. Do you get the amazing beauty of this? Here was a genius of a man who was so spiritual and, yet, he was very playful as a partner. It was a joy to be around someone like that, who showed his love so freely, and he wasn't afraid to express his quirks and unusual talents.

Mutual Respect

As a husband, Dave was respectful of me as an equal. He always took my feelings into consideration. He was also affectionate, kind, attentive, considerate, and caring, which are the qualities that people often overlook. By "considerate," I mean that he included me in his decisions. He collaborated with me, and he trusted my judgment. I would say, "I don't know what to do, Dave." He would tell me, "Just use your common sense, Suzie."

Whenever we talked about something, he treated me as capable. He never looked down on me. He respected me and what I was bringing to a situation. He always asked my opinion on things because it was important to him. Even though he had a long list of accomplishments and a very high intelligence, he valued *my* wisdom too. I think we worked well together because we had that basic respect for each other.

In the morning, when he woke up, we would sit and talk. I loved this time with him. We talked about what project he wanted to work on next ... where we were going to speak ... finances ... everything going on with the office ... how he wanted me to handle certain things in the future. It was like a meeting of minds. We did this every single morning.

People say it's hard for a married couple to live together and work together. I have friends that don't want their husbands to retire because he'll be home all day. They say, "I don't want him to retire—he'll be under my feet all day!" Dave and I were with each other most of the time. The office was in our home, and he wrote his books in the living room, so we lived and breathed the work every day. I think it brought us closer together.

He valued my instinct, which he called "women's intuition." In all the years we were together, there was only one major instance when he did not follow my intuition, and he deeply regretted it and apologized for it. Even the best marriages are not perfect. Both of us were always quick to apologize if we ever made a mistake with each other.

We were two who became one—which is a rarity. Dave liked to say we were "paddling the same canoe." He moves, I move. He talks, I talk. He takes a step, I take a step. We were in sync with each other. We knew what the other one was thinking, without verbally saying it. We had a way of communicating without words. We just looked at each other and that was the joy; there were no words that had to be spoken.

We also gave each other space when we needed it. There were times when I knew that I shouldn't talk to him, when I needed to leave him alone to work on something inside himself. If he was writing a book, or he was working on what he wanted to say for a lecture, he needed to be left alone to let his thoughts come. And there were times when I needed space to take care of things, like with my family members—talking on the phone with siblings, going to visit my mother, other responsibilities I had. Dave understood and respected the range of commitments I had. We each had "outside" problems we had to deal with, in terms of personal or family relationships. We gave each other space to deal with those in the way we thought best. He didn't tell me what to do, and I didn't tell him what to do.

Thoughtfulness and Kindness

As a husband, Dave was loving and thoughtful. He knew me, and he had a way of coming up with special little things to make me happy. He was always very conscious of making *me* happy. As the saying goes, "happy wife, happy life." We laughed at that axiom quite a bit.

He liked to surprise me. I never knew what he might do! Even in the last year of his life, when he couldn't drive any more or see very well, he got me something special for my birthday. He knew I loved jewelry, so he secretly arranged with one of our friends to get me a beautiful hand-crafted Native American necklace. For a Christmas present one year, he gave me plane tickets to Mexico so we could go watch the whales. Christmas was his favorite time of the year because of all the good and giving that comes out of humanity. If he could have his way, it would be Christmas all year. He embodied that spirit of Christmas, no matter what time of year it was.

The kindness and thoughtfulness went both ways. Anything he wanted, he got, and I was happy about it. I didn't look at it as a sacrifice. I was being who I am. Whatever made *him* happy made me happy. You can probably guess that Dave was a very even-keeled person who didn't have a lot of wants—except espresso! We joked that he lived off of espresso and Diet Pepsi, so a good bit of my time every day was making espresso. I made espresso until I thought it was coming out of my ears. He drank it first thing in the morning, and he drank it cold all day. It's what kept him going. At one time, I think we had four or five espresso machines in our tiny kitchen!

Another thing he liked was that I made a cake for his birthday from a special recipe his grandmother handed down. It took the better part of two days to make this cake, but to see the joy and smile on his face made every second worthwhile. We did little things like this, whenever we could, to make each other happy.

We were also affectionate with each other. I knew he loved me because he was very expressive as a partner. He wasn't afraid to show his feelings or give me a "smooch," as we called it. We were open and transparent, and always knew where we stood with each other. A little kiss, a big laugh, and a loving hug go a long way.

Prayer

David was always in prayer, asking for knowledge of God's will for his life and the power to carry it out. The first thing he did before he got out of bed was to say a prayer for that day and what it was going to produce. And the last thing he did at night, lying in bed, was to pray for people and animals that he knew were in difficulty. So, he devoted both the morning and evening to prayer. He taught me that habit. When you do it every day, it becomes your habit.

Often, we would pray together while we did a back exercise. We would lie on our stomachs and pull the upper body up onto the elbows. And we would pray for people, for their relief of suffering. We would pray for our people to understand what we were presenting at the lectures. And if there had been a question that day, we would pray for those people to heal or have what they needed for their situation. We would pray for people who were having difficulties of all kinds.

At night, we would lie down and say prayers for everybody. That is a nice way to end the day, and then you go into a peaceful sleep. It was something we always did. We prayed for any requests that came in from the day on email or phone calls, to pray for people who needed help. We prayed for people who were ill and for the everyday trials that people had to deal with in their lives, their pain and suffering. He always prayed for the pain and the suffering of other people, no matter how minor it might be. Those were some of the spiritual moments we shared together.

One prayer I'll never forget was for a baby fawn that was limping. We saw it at our cabin in the woods. There was a mother deer and two fawns, and one of them was limping. When we left the cabin, Dave said, "I am going to pray for that little fawn." So, all week long he prayed for this little fawn at night. The next time we saw it, the fawn was walking fine. This makes me weep whenever I think of it.

When Dave would see things on TV that moved him, like the people that were going through a hurricane or floods or whatever, he would pray for them. In my life now, I find myself saying a prayer for someone I see on television who is going through hardship, like a child who is ill or dying, or someone who was shot. I say a prayer while I'm watching the news. Some people might say the news is "depressing" or "it's so awful to have all that violence," but, they are still souls, and they need to have someone pray for them.

"Live your life like a prayer" is one of Dave's teachings. And that is exactly what he did. What does that mean to you, to "live your life like a prayer"? For Dave, in his daily life, it meant surrendering everything to God. The bottom line of prayer is to turn your whole life over to God. People want to know what his last words were. To the very end, he was saying to me, "What do you need me to do?" There he was, so physically weak, lying in his hospice bed, but he wanted to be helpful to others. He would say, "I should be doing something—what can I do?" His whole life was that total surrender. He felt fulfilled and happy to be of service. His life was dedicated to helping mankind, individuals and the whole.

I learned from him how to "live your life like a prayer." It's living with compassion for others, stopping in your busy schedule and saying, "Go ahead of me in line." You never know what you're doing for someone in their day, when you say or do something kind. I was in the grocery store the other day, and a little lady came up to me and I could tell she was distressed. And, so, I stopped for a moment to say something to her and make her laugh. She said, "That felt so good. I haven't laughed in a long time."

You don't know what is going on for people, and you might be making their day better just by some gesture or smile or courtesy for them. Dave taught me to be considerate of others, to be kind to all of life. You'll find that it comes back to you in countless ways.

Handling Conflicts

If Dave and I had a disagreement, it was almost always from an outside factor and not something between us. Whatever it was, we could talk it through. We knew how to put emotions to the side. We were careful never to hurt the feelings of the other. I can't ever remember a time when he lost his temper at me. We didn't argue with each other, but sometimes we had disagreements that we had to talk through. It wasn't an argument; it was more of a discussion on how to handle something.

One of the first disagreements that came up was that he wanted me to call him "Doc." Everyone called him "Doc." He said to people, "Don't call me 'guru' or 'teacher' - just call me Doc."

He didn't want a title. "Doc" was what he thought was best. One day he said to me, "Everybody calls me Doc, but you don't. Why?" I said, "Because you're David to me. You will always be David to me." And that was the end of it. He never asked me about it again.

Yes, he was a teacher to me, and I was always learning from him. But he was also something more on a personal level, so it didn't feel right to refer to him as Doc. I sometimes do it when I'm talking with people who are his students because he is "Doc" to them, but usually I say "Dave" or "David." And he had a nickname for me. He always called me "Suzie," and he is the only person that ever called me a nickname. That was his special name for me. So, we both had special names that we called each other. It was an endearment between us that we alone shared. My family called me Susan, and especially my mom insisted I would be called Susan and not any nickname. So, when Dave called me Suzie, it was unique.

Another of our disagreements was about his shirts. Of course, it turned out to be funny, and he joked about it in the lectures. He had his favorite shirts that he wore until they had holes in them. They were as "hole-y" as you could get. When he put the shirts on, he could hardly find the right neck hole because there were so many other holes! I tried to get the shirts repaired, but there was no way. The material had worn so thin, you couldn't sew the holes. So, he relented and said he wouldn't wear shirts with holes in them out in public, like to the doctor's office or around town. He agreed to wear them just around the house. He couldn't see how bad they were, and it was embarrassing to me for him to go around in public wearing raggedy clothes. He respected my feelings about it. Finally, we found another shirt that was soft and comfortable. Clothing had to be super soft and super comfortable, or he would not wear it. It was one of his little quirks that we had to live with.

Dave and I rarely had a problem between us. If we got into a disagreement, it was usually due to something "out there." As the work grew, Dave and I were surrounded by many different personalities, and that's what created stress in our life, more than anything else. We worked to understand why this person does this because of their personality, and why that person does that because of their personality. When you have people working for you, or volunteers, their problems become your problems, especially in a small office and in a small town.

Years ago, there was someone around us that was difficult to deal with. I would say to Dave, "I don't want to deal with this person anymore." And he'd say, "Okay. All right." But that was it. Nothing changed. So, I had to be patient and let it take its course. Then one day, the person came in and flung a report at Dave, and he said, "Do you know they flung a report at me? It is disrespectful. We have to make a change." My ego had been impatient, saying, "We gotta do something, we gotta do something." But that incident taught me that sometimes you have to sit back and let a situation take the form that it needs to take for it to be resolved in the right timing, rather than react immediately to go against it. In other words, let it come to a natural end. That difficult person, in effect, "hung" their own self, as we say; it became so obvious that we had to make a change and so we did.

Dave was kind and easy-going, but if he was pushed, or if someone was disrespectful, he would find a way to end the relationship. It took a lot for him to end it with someone he was close with, but it did happen. He would never retaliate, but he would walk away from the relationship, leaving it to karma to handle the situation.

He taught me that, first of all, you don't know what's going on with that person, so you can't condemn them. You have to surrender them to their own karma. And, second, you don't want to go down to their level by responding in kind. He was tested, even with his closest people. He would usually give a person many chances and do everything he could to address the problems in a positive way. But, if the negativity continued, he knew he had to end it. I learned from him that sometimes you have to let go, even of the people closest to you. It doesn't do any good to fight back; it's best just to walk away and let karma take its own course.

He was a very patient, considerate and caring person to live with. I don't know if it's the norm for an advanced spiritual being to be like that, but that's my experience living with someone who, to me, was enlightened. The downfall was that sometimes people took advantage of him, and that was very hard for me to witness. He tended to see only the good in people who wanted something from him. As he got older, he was more vulnerable in that way, to be taken advantage of, because his eyesight was weak. The worst betrayal happened toward the end of his life, and he deeply regretted the mistake of trusting someone he should not have.

Dave's intention was always sincere. That's what he taught us. If your intention is sincere, then making a mistake is not a problem; you learn from it. But if your intention is to get something for your own self, then that greed will come back to get you.

Dave saw the innocence of everything and that's why he didn't judge anyone for what they were. On the other hand, he also taught that you don't welcome negative people into your home. Like Dave said, "You see the innocence, but you don't allow it to walk around in your house." He often reminded us of Jesus's teaching to avoid negative people. Don't attack them, and don't make them "wrong." They can't help how they are. Just avoid them. Of course, this can be hard if they are relatives or people we work with. In that case, he taught, we have to transcend our attachment to them. If people are non-integrous, they have a negative energy and it's not good to hang around with that. In his August 2002 lecture, he put it this way:

Non-integrous people are a doorway through which the energies of that which is non-integrous now have a play with your life. So, it's more that you want to plug up the hole, the leak. It's that they're a leak, and through them come all kinds of things. Your brakes fail, battery goes dead, the ceiling begins to leak. You wonder where the hell is all this coming from?!....You can love the cobra for its intrinsic beauty, for that which it is, but you can't really let him run around the house. Why? Because you're going to sit in your chair someday and forget the cobra is there, and [slaps hands together]- goodbye, there you go. [Laughter.] .... A cobra bite in the tail is always fatal, you know.

In the leg, it's okay, but a cobra bite there, it's goodbye! So, you can't have a cobra in the house because you might sit on it … So, the non-integrous brings into your life the unwanted result, and it does it innocently by nature of its own energy of which it is unaware.

It's a choice to let that which is non-integrous go from one's life. In many peoples' spiritual evolution, this is a crucial area. Crucial area. And we see many people in a town like Sedona, for instance, who leave everything, and everyone, and all their titles, and buildings, and money, and relationships, and everything. They give up everything for God, and then, they drive a bus to make ends meet! So, we see the willingness to sacrifice everything for God. And whatever it is, if it is non-integrous, it *has* to go, sooner or later. It has to go. And it's sort of a test. The willingness to surrender everything to God…. One may have to walk away from one's own child and surrender that to God. "Well, God, he's your problem now."

David saw the good in everybody, which was his Achilles heel. When you are so kind and so giving, it brings up the opposite. People come to take advantage of you. It was a fine line that he lived. He loved people. He loved the work. He loved God. And then sometimes we got hit with the opposite of that.

We could always tell when we were getting hit with some kind of negative energy, because mechanical things would malfunction—the water well, the septic tank, the computers, the car, the irrigation system, etc. He called it "abraxic energy," which is chaotic energy, and he would say his prayers. I was smudging and doing incense all the time to safeguard the energy in the house. We had very few disagreements between us, but there was a lot of negative energy that came at us from the outside. I'm sure that is why he had been so hesitant to write books and lecture. As soon as you put yourself out into the world, you have to deal with people who want to use you, ride your coattails, distort your work, attack you, and all of that.

Calm and Patient

Dave was calm and patient no matter what was happening. As a partner, this is a wonderful trait to have, because it helps the person you're with to feel secure. If you panic, how does that help anyone? Dave knew how to stay calm in a crisis.

Here's an example. In 2005, we decided that we wanted to visit Alaska. Neither one of us had been there. Dave was tired of making huge trips, but he knew that going to Alaska meant a lot to me. It was one of the last trips we made together, and it was incredible. We took in everything beautiful you can imagine. We saw whales and dall sheep, we took a helicopter ride over the glaciers, and we visited Kodiak island.

On the return trip, something bizarre happened. The cruise ship started having electrical problems. One whole side of the ship's electrical pod went down, and it felt like the ship was listing to one side. We were on the top level and the elevators weren't working. The ship became very unstable. Doors were banging and everything was off-kilter. Every time a wave crashed, it felt like the whole ship was being broken in two!

I was scared. Dave said to me in a calm voice, "You know, I think we should just hang our life vest on the back of the chair here. Just in case." He did it in such a way that I felt assured. He had a way of presenting himself to you that you were never fearful. It was just so calm the way he said it. He had been a sailor in World War II and survived a typhoon, so I knew he knew what he was talking about. He said, "Just so that we know right where they are, in case in the middle of the night we get called out and have to leave the ship." What he said sort of unsettled me—"leave the ship"? "middle of the night"?—but he said it in such a way that it made me feel like everything would be okay. And it was. The next morning, I was standing out on the balcony and saw the big tugboat come to stabilize our ship and pull us out. Our cruise ship limped into port and everybody disembarked, relieved to be on land! I will never forget Alaska because of how Dave was so calm during that crisis.

Questions and Answers

Q: What was the best part of living with Doc?

A: His humor! Oh, he was so funny. You have no idea. When I was having a bad day, he always said something that made me laugh, and it lifted me right out of my bad day. And he would let his little boy come out. He was very playful. Sometimes I would tell him, "Let your little boy come out and play!" We had so much fun.

Also, he taught me to be aware of life around me. We live on a small ranch with about 30 chickens, and we have ducks who live on the pond. We used to have llamas, but we had to give them to a rescue farm because we couldn't handle the work anymore. If you watch nature, you can learn from it. That's what Dave taught me. For example: the pecking order of the chicken coop. If you look at it, you'll see human behavior, how one chicken will pick on another, or how one chicken is a better egg layer than another. If you watch nature, you learn about yourself and humankind. If you watch cats, you see them fighting with each other, and one is more dominant than the other, so you can see human behavior in that dynamic. You just have to be aware of what you're seeing.

That's kind of like with miracles, you have to be aware that you're witnessing a miracle. And you have to stop and say, "That was a small miracle that happened just then!" Dave and I did that all the time. We had an amazing life. I'm grateful for it.

Q: Is there a little practice that you could give those of us who are married? I am trying to walk this spiritual pathway, but I find that anger is coming up, impatience, criticism, judgmentalism. What do I do with all of this?

A: You want to try to put those emotions to the side, because it has nothing to do with you. It has to do with the spiritual work. And that's what I had to learn. If my emotions were there, if I was frustrated or feeling lost, I had to put those to the side. It had to do with what Dave was here to accomplish, and I knew that. So, I had to help any way I could, whether it was cooking meals, picking up, whatever I had to do, I did it. And that was part of who I was. You become part of who that person is that you're living with, too. So, it's a respect in exchange. I got frustrated sometimes, but I tried my best to work it out in myself.

Dave and I hardly ever fought. The one time I remember, we were having an issue with something, and I was heated up, so I got in the car, and I went to see a movie. I didn't want to say anything rash or hurtful to Dave. The movie was called *City of Angels*. That was the best movie I could have seen, because by the end of it, I had lost my anger! When I got back home, he said, "Why did you leave before we worked it out?" I said, "Because I was afraid that I was going to say something that I didn't want to say." I didn't want to hurt his feelings. I didn't want to say something I'd regret later. So, if I had those feelings, it was better just to take myself away for a while, so that I wouldn't do that. And the movie, of course, is all about someone passing on and how they adjust to it and an angel coming back to the earth. It's a good movie. And I realized that I was going to have to give up what I thought I needed in order to make our work together happen. So, I had sacrifices, but it wasn't really a sacrifice. It was more like a giving of myself to help things go forward. I guess that's what I need to say. It was not a sacrifice; it was more of a giving for the greater good. So maybe we can practice giving more of ourselves to make the people around us happy.

Q: What's something you learned from living with Doc that you can pass on to us?
A: He loved mankind and his whole life was devoted to helping mankind to understand what is truly important, which is the spiritual self, the soul. He passed that along to all of us, that our soul is the only thing we take with us. In the end that's all we take. Nothing else matters.

So, then, what are we as human beings supposed to be doing here on earth? Dave taught us to be kind. And I think as human beings this means to just be there when someone didn't ask you to be there—just being there, when someone needs a friend or needs help. They don't even have to need it. Just be there and let them know that you're there and everything's going to be okay. Kindness is one of those beautiful things. I think it was Mark Twain, who made a quote that I really like: "Kindness is a language in which the deaf can hear and the blind can see."

Dave taught me about kindness, and that it always comes back to you. I remember one time, it was Veterans Day, and we had gone out to breakfast. There were four people with us, all women. Dave wore his Veteran's hat. We were sitting there having breakfast and everybody was laughing, talking and having a good time. Dave was being Dave, telling stories. It came time to pay for the check, so I went up to pay for it. The owner of the restaurant said, "You don't owe anything. It has been taken care of. Someone paid for it." I was shocked. I went back and told Dave. He walked up to the owner and said, "Thank you, and whoever it was, please thank him for me." We were both very moved. It was such a great feeling to have someone acknowledge him for being in World War II. I passed it along, to pay it forward. That person's kindness, to pay for our breakfast like that, to honor Dave's service, it rippled out way beyond that.

CHAPTER 5

LIVING WITH AN ENLIGHTENED BEING

Dave was a private, humble man. He never would have said, "I'm enlightened." To him, enlightenment is a *condition* or a *state of consciousness*, not a person, not an identity. It certainly was not a title or an achievement. It's a label many people put on him.

Of course, people had their own ideas about what it was like to live with him. One woman asked me, "What's it like to live with an enlightened being who can read your mind?" I said, "If he could read my mind, then I'd have new carpet in the house!" I don't think that's the answer she expected!

Even if he had been able to "read my mind," Dave never would have used that in our relationship. He didn't say to me or anybody, "I have special powers. I am an enlightened being." I saw him live at that level, but he was very humble and down-to-earth. He didn't see himself as any better than anyone else. He just knew he had a responsibility to share what he was and to help the world any way that he could.

What is an Enlightened Being?

In his books and lectures, Dave described the states of enlightenment and what occurred in his experience, so I won't repeat it here except to remind us of one thing. It happens *spontaneously*. He wanted us to remember that. Dave said it's not something that you yourself can "make happen." It's what you have *become* as a consequence of Divine Will and Divine Grace. It occurs of its own when the time is right, and it has nothing to do with *you.*

That's why he was always humble about what he was. He knew there was no personal self that had anything to do with it! When that condition came on, his personal self was wiped out, so who would be the one to say, "I am enlightened"? It would have been absurd.

One of Dave's favorite jokes at the lectures was, "I've got more humility than anybody I know!" He liked to make us laugh at the ego and how it wants to be the best. In truth, he *was* the humblest person you could ever meet.

As I shared before, I had my own glimpse into that higher state. He called it a "gift from Divinity." We were at a lecture (May 2011) and he wanted me to describe my experience and then he calibrated it in the 600s on the Map of Consciousness®. He said it was the experience of seeing the Beauty and Divinity of all that exists, and it was given as a gift. In other words, I wasn't thinking, "I want to be enlightened" or "I hope I have a high experience today," and so forth. I was just driving home from town one day, and WOOSH! All of a sudden, the rocks came alive, and they were breathing; the whole scene turned into 3-D, and I witnessed the vibrant aliveness of Creation.

After he told the audience of my experience, Dave said: "That's why we call enlightenment a 'gift.' It's not something that you earned, acquired or paid for. It's a gift from Divinity. Suddenly you walk along the street, it lights up, and you see the miraculous." So, I learned from him that these states are *spontaneous.* They are a "gift" and a "revelation," he said.

That brief glimpse of 3-D reality gave me an inkling into his inner world, even though for me it lasted only a minute or so. What was it like for him actually to *live* there, and then to go beyond to even higher realms? I won't know until I get there. I can only share with you what it was like to live with him in the states he was in. It was extremely hard on him to be in those higher states and then to keep on existing as a human being.

Dave said he had three options. One, he could leave the world. He liked to joke, "No one gets out of here alive!" In the state of enlightenment, one is happy to leave the world, and he said that most people do. You're not a personal self anymore, and you no longer identify with a body, and so the world holds no personal attraction. He came close to leaving many times, but he never could get out of here! He had to complete his work.

Two, he could live in a monastery or ashram and exist like Ramana Maharshi did, sitting there and blessing people who came for that Presence. Dave had done that kind of lifestyle in other lifetimes, being in monasteries, living like a sadhu dying by the Ganges River. This time around, it wasn't his destiny to live in that insulated way.

Or, three, he could come back into the world to share that energy with the rest of us. That's what he did. He returned to the world *solely* out of love for others and as a servant of the Lord. I can't emphasize that enough. His whole life was devoted to relieving the suffering of others. He did that first as a physician, and then he did it as a spiritual teacher.

People ask me, "What's it like to live with a mystic?" For one thing, his states varied. Isn't that true for all of us? People have a false notion that the levels of consciousness are static and linear, but they are not. For example, when Dave wrote his books, he went through different states, depending on the book he was writing. His books calibrate at different levels, and he was in different states when he wrote them. He worked hard to express his teachings through different levels. He felt that responsibility as a teacher. He wanted everyone to have what they needed, which required him to express the teachings at different levels.

I: Reality and Subjectivity was the hardest book for him to write because it is from such a high state. When he was writing that book, he was "spacey." Even though he could do ordinary activities like pick up a coffee cup, drink the coffee, and set it back down—I knew he wasn't there when he was doing it! When he went into that kind of space, he was not of the body.

When he was writing *Truth vs. Falsehood,* it was different. He was trying to apply the teachings to the many facets of society, so he was more engaged in the world. Many people think that if you are spiritual, you shouldn't be concerned with the world, or that there shouldn't be wars and so forth. But Dave said that there has been some sort of war in most of human history. This is not a heavenly realm! So, he wanted to provide a book that helped us understand the world and its conflicts. In order to do that, he had to go back into the world and trace its conflicts. For example, what were the levels of consciousness of the different people and factors in World War II? This might help us know what to look for in future conflicts. He laid out the dynamics of the world for people like us, who are not at his same enlightened level.

Not everybody's at the same place on the Map of Consciousness®. I hear people say they want to try for the higher states, but it doesn't work like that. You have to accept where you are at the time, not try to be "higher" than where you are. Some people want to *force* becoming enlightened, and that's the ego wanting to *get* something. "If I do this or act like this, then I'll be at a high calibration!" Dave said not to see the Map as a scorecard or a measuring stick. I never heard him say, "Look how far I've come!" He was always saying, "What can I work on in myself so I can help someone else?" It's not a race to see who can climb up the Map faster! We're all in this together to help each other evolve. Are you willing to serve just as you are?

Handling the High States

Living with Dave presented some unique challenges. Sometimes, all of a sudden, he would go into a high state and become incapacitated. When that happened, he would just stand there. His eyes would glass over, and he couldn't move. I wasn't able to talk to him in that state; he couldn't register verbiage. So, I literally had to take him by his hand and lead him to where he needed to be. Sometimes this state would come on if he looked at something or somebody and picked up their essence. The beauty of it just knocked him out. I had to watch out for those times and take care of him. It would happen when we drove back and forth to the cabin, a couple hours away. The scenery is beautiful. We'd put on opera or beautiful music and, suddenly, that state would take over.

When Dave was in those higher states, he couldn't track anything linear *at all*. Most people can connect one thing with another thing, and understand how they might fit together, but he couldn't do that. For him, the two things were entirely separate. Whereas to me, the two things were clearly connected, he just did not see it that way. Instead, he saw each thing in its own box, its own dimension. For example, he did not connect the two ideas of: "When it's time for the lecture to start, I need to walk to the podium." So, I had to make sure that I, or someone, was there to guide his body to the right place on stage. For Dave, when it required physical movement to do something, that's when he had the hardest time, because he was not *with* the physical body. He was everywhere, in everything—that was his perspective. "There is only one Self," he said, and he saw the Self radiating from everyone and everything. He didn't see separateness; he saw Allness. When you don't see yourself as separate from anything or anyone else, how do you manage in a world that is based on separateness? That was his challenge.

Over the years, he learned how to act "normal" most of the time. He could interact with people so that they *thought* a "person," David, was there. In reality, he was not identified with his body but with the Presence. He said the Holy Spirit helped him with communication. He would joke, "I can fool most of the people most of the time." But he couldn't fool *me*. If he started to slip into that state, I knew it. If he was in a really high state, he'd come and look at me in a certain way. And then I had to literally move him to where he needed to be. It happened a lot when he was writing about the high states.

I remember, one time, we were at home and not doing anything in particular. He always had his can of Diet Pepsi and his espresso nearby. He was just sitting there, and I noticed he got really quiet. I felt a shift in the room. I looked over at him and he was totally glassed over. He was not there—he was in a different realm. I don't know what triggered it, and I never asked him, because it was his experience and I knew there were no words for it.

In those states, I found it was best to leave him be, to let him do what he was doing, and I would go on about the day. He would be very quiet, just sitting there. You could go up to him and wave your hand in front of his face and it wouldn't affect him. It's like he was glazed over. He wouldn't see your hand or anything else. He said it was like being in slow motion. The sense of time wasn't there.

If I wasn't pressed by other things, I would stop and sit with him. It was a nice relief to sit there and be in that space with him. But usually, I had a lot of tasks to take care of. We had so much going on with the events, books, and all of the correspondence. People were always emailing or calling with questions.

I had to learn patience. In any given day, we had several decisions that we needed to discuss, but it wasn't always possible for him to do that. At times, I had to wait days to discuss things with him, and sometimes they were pressing questions. But he wasn't able to connect the dots, so I just had to wait. I never knew what state he was going to wake up to. I wanted him to have that time because it was a completely restful state for him. Whenever those blissful states came on, I did my very best not to interrupt.

Patience was the most important virtue needed with Dave. Sometimes I had to let go of getting things done in a timely manner, because I had to wait on him to discuss them. I might feel frustrated with the timing, but when I thought about the state he was in, my frustration became meaningless. So, I just said, "Okay, he can't handle it today. That's all there is to it."

Some people ask, "Didn't you want to go there and be in that state too?" It is a beautiful state, and my time will come, but someone needed to take care of all the details in the world, such as keeping the espresso machine pumping and getting the books printed! My feeling was, "This is *his* time right now. My time will come—maybe not in this lifetime but another one." I know that it will. It will happen for anyone in some lifetime if that's what they really, really desire with all their heart.

Sometimes, when he was speaking, he would say a certain phrase, and I could feel that aura coming in. When he was talking about the Presence, that Presence was suddenly there, and I could feel it. It felt almost like angels surrounded him, or the Presence of a Divine Being, and he became engulfed by the Divine State.

We lived with the fact that he might leave his body during a public lecture, and not come back. In other words, talking about the Divine States brought them on, and it was hard for him to come back after that. I was afraid he was going to bliss out and not be able to talk any more. And then what would we do? He can't give a lecture in that state! How would people react? And that's what he was afraid of, too. As I mentioned, we had one of those moments during our lecture in February, 2003. That state came on, and it was so strong, he almost left the body to die. He said he was given the choice on whether to leave or not leave. For him, death wasn't a reality at all. But he knew that I would be distraught if he died right there, and that all the people would be upset. He let go of wanting to leave the world many times, so he could remain here and fulfill his commitment to help all of us.

Even now, as I try to describe it, I wish I could find the words. I can see why so few mystics stay in the world. Most of them leave the world, or if they stay, they have a hard time finding the words to express their experience. The fact that Dave was able to do that verbalization is incredible. It was only possible because of Divine Will and Divine Grace. He always gave 100% credit to the Lord. He began and ended his books and lectures with *Gloria in Excelsis Deo!* "Glory to God Most High."

Inner Work - Wracking Pain

The higher realms come with intense physical pain and discomfort. I don't think this is commonly known. People think, "Oh I want to be enlightened! I want to reach those higher states!" But they don't know what they're asking for! They think it's blissful and beatific all the time.

Yes, in some states, it *is* bliss and ecstasy. Dave talked about the high 500s as being magical. He saw the Divine Light radiating out of everything. He had an exquisite energy of love that ran up his spine and out of his heart to enter car wrecks on the side of the highway to help someone who had been praying. It's like he was an antenna of God's Love, and this exquisite energy ran through him to heal people and situations. He said he did not perform the miracles. Divinity just used his aura as a conduit for healing energy to be poured out to others when needed.

Some of our novice students, when they hear about Dave's blissful states, get this childlike fantasy that they'll be transported into a magical state. Their ego even produces that very fantasy; their eyes roll to the back of their head and they swoon. They become quite demonstrative with their supposed "high state"!

The path of enlightenment is not a yellow brick road of bliss! I saw Dave go through intense physical pain in the higher realms. He had to confront major blocks in the collective consciousness of mankind. For Dave, the slightest thing that was "out," or negative, brought on a wracking pain throughout his whole nervous system. He said that his bones ached as if they were crushed, and his nerves were on fire, like barbed wire running through his body, as if electrocuting him. I can't imagine anything more excruciating than that! It would go on within his whole aura, and so he couldn't get away from it.

I've heard people say they want to be where Dave was on the Map. But I'm here to tell you, it is no picnic in the park! He went through agonizing pain because he was always working in himself to clear whatever he could from past lifetimes, and to clear things in the collective consciousness. It's like he carried the weight for all of us. He was willing to use his high consciousness to help clear out negativities from the collective. When something non-integrous (below 200 on the Map) would suddenly hit him, he'd lie there in pain. Or he'd be zapped with exhaustion. He could often intuit what it was, or we'd use the arm to pinpoint what it was. And then he would clear it.

In one of his lectures (May 2011), he said: "You take on things from the collective consciousness, things that people cannot clear for themselves. So, you try to take advantage of whatever capacity you have still remaining, to clear what you can for all of mankind."

He said that from level 700 on up, a teacher is in the state of Self-Realization and able to tackle the blocks in the collective consciousness of mankind in order to transcend them. Each level confronts us with a paradox to transcend. When the teacher gets beyond the level of 800 or so, he said, it can be extremely painful to the physical body. This is where the mystic will end up. One of the biggest paradoxes he had to resolve was "existence versus non-existence." It comes up at level 835, and he was wracked with pain at this level. In his July 2002 lecture, he told us:

> As you get beyond the 700s, it becomes almost beyond the doable. The strain of the energy, the constant pain, the sort of agonizing feeling of hot wires being ripped out of your nervous system all the time. Any kind of negativity that you hold within your consciousness, it's just like you got put in the electric chair and they got it ten volts below "kill," you know? And you've got to find out what that is; you've got to clear that with very intense prayer; and only with the help of the Holy Spirit does it even resolve. So, it's arduous.... It's a ferocity—to grit and walk through the day with this agonizing, almost paralyzing pain; to act and behave normally and at the same time searching what it is in you that's out. Is it coming from out there? Is it coming from within you? Is it coming from your own karma? Is it coming from the collective? You have to try and track down the origin of it.

He said that each level comes with a paradox that has to be resolved. That's what he wrote about in *Transcending the Levels of*

Consciousness. He laid out the dualities that we have to transcend at each level of consciousness.

Even on our level, though we're not in that higher realm, we know when we're "stuck." We call it a "block," don't we? There's some positionality that we have to get beyond, in order to evolve to the next level. We might have emotional or physical pain until it's resolved. Maybe we feel bad over something we said, and we're stuck in guilt until we have the humility to apologize. Or maybe we're angry at someone, and we're stuck in that resentment until we can forgive. It's a great release of energy when we can finally let go of a positionality.

For Dave, he was at an extremely high level, and so when he was "stuck," his level of discomfort was extreme. And he was bearing that pain not for himself, but for all of mankind. When we were in Korea, and he had that agonizing pain that I mentioned earlier, he said he was hit with "a seeming duality" that had to be transcended (January 2002 Lecture). His dedication to Divinity was so high that it pulled up its opposite, or "seeming" opposite as he would say. Even in the last year of his life, he was working through some final purifications.

Transcending the levels of consciousness as a mystic is not for the faint-hearted. From watching Dave, I would say it's the most demanding of any human experience.

Questions and Answers

Q: Doc mentioned in some of his lectures that he spent a lot of time out of his body when he was living by himself during his early years in Arizona. Were there any kinds of those experiences that you saw while you were living with him? Did you ever stumble across his physical body in the house?
A: No, it wasn't like that. He was in a different space. In the period you are referring to, which is before I met him, he was doing a lot of meditation. He told me what happened one time. He'd been out of body for one or two days. He said, "I went and

looked in the mirror and was surprised to see someone! 'Oh, who is that?!'" Then he realized he was looking at himself in the mirror! He was working through different inner states when he lived alone. Then, when he moved to the ranch, he had some other high experiences. He told me about one that happened when he was out in the yard, and he just lay down on the ground because he thought he was leaving his body. Buzzards were circling around him. Then all of a sudden, he got up and said, "Guess it wasn't time to go!"

He did have experiences like that, where he was present but not in the body. It was like someone in a trance, I would say. If you've ever experienced a very high state, you know it's impossible to *live* there. It's like you have been given a glimpse of something higher than where you are. Enjoy it because you're not going to be able to stay there. Dave gives us the example of what it takes to stay there. It's a *lot* of inner work, and you go through a lot of inner anguish and physical pain. That's what it takes to *become* that state.

Dave also advised that when a divine state takes over, you should be in a monastery, an ashram or some very protected place, like Ramana Maharshi was. You shouldn't be living by yourself, which Dave was at that earlier time.

I've heard stories about him from before I knew him. He was walking down the street, and he didn't even recognize a friend of his who was walking down the road to see him. He walked right by her. She was upset because he didn't recognize her, but he was in a deep contemplation working through an inner question.

During this time, he wasn't eating very much. People would come to him and say, "Do you want to go out for lunch? Have you eaten today?" And he hadn't, so they said, "Come on, we'll go to lunch." People would do that for him. The doors opened, and he was being taken care of, because he was supposed to stay in that state for a certain length of time, so that he could write about it. That's my sense of it. I think he had to experience all those different states, so that he could tell us about it and let us know what it takes to reach those divine states of consciousness.

His example gives us a lesson that we can achieve anything we want, spiritually, but we have to work on it. And also, he didn't do it for himself. He did it out of his love for God and for mankind. His inner work was a service. In the end, we're all responsible for our own spiritual awareness. We'll get where we want to go—eventually, maybe years, maybe lifetimes. But we have a responsibility for own spiritual nourishment. We're all responsible for ourselves. Some people want it to be given to them – "This guy's going to take me there. If I just do this, then it will happen." Dave's example is that he worked nonstop on himself, and he was willing to surrender everything to do it. Can we say the same?

Q: Did he choose to come back to share?
A: Yes and no. Yes, he knew he had to teach. But it's hard to describe because there was no "person" that exactly decided. I guess I would say that there was something in him that made an agreement to come back and teach. And there was something in me that agreed to help him fulfill it.

He said that our students are dedicated to enlightenment. "That's why you are here in this class," he would say. "You are the future 'mystics' in this lifetime or the next." We had to create this body of work for those that needed it.

I asked him one time, "How many lifetimes did you have?" He said, "Many." I asked him why he came back, and he said, "I didn't have to come back in this lifetime. I did it because I had to teach people about what they were to become. I came back for that purpose only." He had to have those experiences so he could tell us what it's like. Where else would you read about it? I think it is very rare to have the kind of personal account of spiritual life that he gave us.

So, my job was to help him be able to do that and reach as many people as he could before his life ended. That was an understanding that we had with each other. I was there to help him succeed in completing the teachings that he knew he had to do. Why that is, I don't know, but it was written long ago. It was just something that

I had to do as a human being. And I also knew that, because of our age difference, I would be here by myself to carry on after he left, and he knew that too. And, so, I do the best I can to keep the work alive. It's constantly a challenge, with all the changes in electronics, going from VHS to DVDs and tape cassettes to CDs, and now to digital. The information channels are always evolving. We had to hire people to do all the changes because it's very technical, and to make master copies of all the work. That is my job, to keep the work alive and to keep it available to the public so that the people who need to find it, will find it.

Q: When did you realize he was a modern-day mystic?
A: I accepted him for who he was, as a partner. And this was part of who he was. A mystic doesn't walk around in white robes and glowing from head to toe. They're constantly working on them-selves. The first clue for me was that Dave was constantly working on his spiritual self, to see things differently. In order to evolve, you have to shift your perspective, to see it from someone else's view-point. And he was always doing that. He would say, "Well, now I understand he saw it from this viewpoint." Several times he said that to me—he saw clearly the way that another person was look-ing at it. That's what a mystic can do. They can shift from seeing it this way, to the way another person was seeing it. It's like they can actually enter into the other person and see it through their eyes. That was the first clue to me that Dave was unusual.

Was he a mystic? For me, yes. But he never put grand labels on himself. We put it on him. He didn't take on the terms of avatar, guru, mystic, and so forth. He was a man with a spiritual quest. And he was humble about it. He couldn't relate to the titles. If you called him Doc, he loved it, but there's no need to add a title on that. How do you explain someone who's highly spiritual like that, other than the term 'mystic'? It's useful as a term, to designate a realm of human experience, but it's just a term.

People get hung up on words. One time, Dave and I were talking about cuss words, which he used frequently. You have to remember that he was a sailor in the Navy! He told me, "Who said that was a bad word that shouldn't be used? Somebody just decided to call it a bad word, but really, it's just a word." He didn't think there was anything bad about using cuss words. He tried not to take God's name in vain, but the others were free for the saying!

People often think that the mystic is someone that you put up on this pedestal, as if they're not human, but they *are* human. He was born into a human body, so he was human. And he had feelings and he had pain. If something heavy dropped on his foot, guess what? He cussed!

Q: Doc talked about some very challenging experiences that he went through, having the level of consciousness that he did. One example that comes to mind is when he talks about feeling there was barbed wire with electricity being run through his body. Most of us get worried about our spouses over minor things, like if they had a bad day at work! What was it like to be his spouse in those kinds of situations?

A: He said it was like his nerves were on fire and his bones were breaking. I mentioned this before but it's worth re-stating. We were in Korea the first time he told me that. He was lying down taking a nap. And I was trying to learn Korean off the TV. I found a book on the Buddha in the drawer, so I opened it up and started reading. And it said that when the Buddha was approaching his enlightenment, he was attacked by demons, his bones felt like they were breaking, and his nerves were on fire. And I said, "David, I know why you're feeling that!" He wanted me to read it to him. And he said, "Thank you, that explains a lot." He never knew what it was.

When your loved one is going through any kind of anguish, you do whatever you can to relieve their suffering. We were both so glad to read that passage about the Buddha. And after that, Dave was better, because he realized that that was part of who he was. I suppose answers like that come when you are ready for them.

After seeing what Dave went through, with so much physical pain, I am not eager to be enlightened. He said he felt like he was being electrocuted—would you want to go through that? I saw the pain that he went through, up close. He said that the human nervous system cannot handle the voltage. That's the way he put it. The voltage is so strong. And it takes many, many lifetimes of serious spiritual devotion and focus to become a high spiritual being like he was. I can see why. You have to be ready to go through that intense pain in your body. Protoplasm has a hard time handling that very high energy. The only reason Dave bore with it is because he knew that energy would be of service to others, and he himself was of service to God.

One method of clearing yourself that Dave used was the "thymus thump," and he taught it to me. If you've been around negative energy or you're having a bad day, you can use the thymus thump. It clears the energy blocks from anything negative. We would do it quite often. He would also use prayer to clear himself.

Q: Did you ever find yourself having to explain to people why he might not recognize them - perhaps people who were not spiritually aware and wouldn't understand why he was that way?
A: No, I didn't make excuses for him. He was who he was. I didn't feel I needed to explain who he was. If they didn't recognize it, that was their problem.

Q: Was there a catalyst that started him on his spiritual journey?
A: Yes, he talks about it. It was that very high state. He was hit like a bolt of lightning, and that's what changed him. He saw the innate beauty of the world, how everything was a total, timeless oneness. He said he would be walking down an alleyway in the streets of New York City, a scene that people saw as ugly, but for him it looked beautiful, like a French impressionist painting. There was the beat-up garbage can, and it was beautiful and perfect in its expression. He was seeing it as if for the first time. Isn't that incredible? It was an old garbage can in an alley, but he was seeing it like it was a sculpture. He said that his whole perception changed

after that enlightenment. He witnessed the Presence of God in everything. He said, "Beauty is inherent to everything."

Sometimes he would talk about the Kleenex coming out of the box and how beautiful it was. He also talked about how you go out into the woods and, all of a sudden, you realize that all the trees are breathing and all the bark on the trees is alive, and every little pine needle has its own place on the tree. When I had that experience, before we started doing lectures, it was a gorgeous day. The clouds were those cotton-like beautiful monsoon clouds in the sky of blue. I wasn't really thinking about anything. All of a sudden, I had to pull over to the side of the road, because it looked as though every wall of rock was breathing. I couldn't believe my eyes. I was seeing the love of Creation, and how beautiful everything is, just as it is.

Q: When he first got hit like that, and saw all of creation in its stunning beauty, did that stick around, or did it fade for him? In his teaching, it sounds like he says that it fades, and you have to build it back up.

A: Let's see... how do I answer that? Yes and no. When it comes, it's a shock. And then you have to go back to everyday life, and be with people and take care of them. But it's always there under the surface. If you wanted to, you could bring that inner state back, but it has to be in a certain setting. You can't do it with a bunch of people around. It's a very personal experience, when you do have that higher experience, and you're never the same. Even though you go back to your "normal" life, that experience stays with you. I want to say it's like a glimpse of the Higher Self. When you have those experiences, it's like a glimpse of what you could become, or what your soul is, or what you really are. You're not afraid anymore. It's like your whole being vibrates with that vibration, and you're a different person. Doc went through many breakthroughs in consciousness. It's always there under the surface. It's within your being, your aura. It's within that inner Self.

Q: What do you recommend for us, if we'd like to reach that mystic state?

A: First of all, let go of trying to "reach" for a spiritual state. That's the ego wanting something special for itself.

Second, Dave would say that it's already right there, you just have to recognize it. He'd be walking in a mall, and a couple would show affection towards each other, and the love that transpired between them, which is simple and ordinary, would just blow him away. He'd weep from the beauty of it. So, if we would just take the time to look at the miracles of love around us at all times, then we'd be there.

Of course, everyday life is so busy. You're cooking, you're cleaning, you're running your businesses, you're taking care of the animals, the kids, whatever you are doing in your daily life, all these wonderful things that we do to keep our lives in order. It's difficult to take that time and just be quiet and observe, but it's important to do that. It's contemplation. And I think that is what Dave was saying, to contemplate nature, or the things around us, and come from our heart. Then kindness comes over you and you feel grateful for everything in your life. We need to be a little bit more grateful. This is my opinion, not Dave's. I think we need to be more grateful for the things that come our way, the little miracles that happen every day.

6

EXTRAORDINARY MAN WHO STROVE TO BE "ORDINARY"

If you had multiple talents and you excelled at all of them, how would you choose your focus in life? If you had the capability to do whatever you wanted in life, would you live for your own personal happiness, or would you live for the greater good?

When I think about Dave's life, he could have done or been anything he'd wanted, but he chose to dedicate his life to helping others. He was a Renaissance man, versatile with many talents—music, carpentry, architecture, inventions, scientific research, business, writing, and more. He played multiple musical instruments, for example. He was extraordinary in many areas of life. Though he never mentioned this in public, his IQ classified him as an exceptional genius.

He ended up choosing to become a psychiatrist so he could help heal the psyches of suffering people. That career took him into the spiritual realm, and he became an author and teacher in the spiritual area, to help raise the level of consciousness of mankind. His entire life was dedicated to relieving the suffering of others. The fact that he chose to help mankind in the areas of healing and spirituality says a lot about what he was.

Extraordinary Man

If you're reading this book, you already know the traits that he is famous for, as an author, physician, and spiritual teacher. I'd like to share a few of the behind-the-scenes traits that made him extraordinary to me.

As you know, Dave and I met in country-western dance class. By the time I met him, he was a very good dancer. If you watched him on the dance floor, you would have said, "Very smooth!" But for most of his life, he was afraid to dance. He was too self-conscious even to try. He said he felt like he had "two left feet." In his lectures, he talked about how fear can shrink our life. It constricts us, holds us back. He would avoid situations where there was dancing. He built up a whole defense around this lifelong fear. Whenever people asked him to dance, he'd say, "I can't dance."

One day, he decided it was time to let go of that fear. He got up and started dancing, and as he moved, he just kept letting go of the fear. In his lectures, he talked about "breaking through that barrier of 'I can't.'" He surrendered to the dance, and then the dance was dancing him. It's like he became one with the very thing that he had spent so many years being afraid of. He loved dancing for the rest of his life.

If he had not been willing to break through his fear of dancing, I might never have met him. If he had stayed in that fear of dancing, would any of us have ever heard him or read his books? Dancing was something that he never thought he could do, and yet he overcame it, and it opened up many other doors for himself and others.

We might ask ourselves, what are we afraid of? Do we have what it takes to break through the barriers? In one of his lectures (July 2002), he told us that we need an inner drive in our spiritual work:

> I think that's where the Sufi dancers discover it, too. And I also discovered it at dancing. There's a certain point in which you stop dancing, and you are being danced.... In serious spiritual work, if a person is really committed to enlightenment, you're going to run up against that barrier, more than once. There's that barrier beyond which you cannot go, and yet, you have to

go beyond it, and you summon up all the spiritual power and intention you have, and by the intention of will and fixity of will, you break through the barrier and the impossible becomes possible.

And that's one of the extraordinary things about Dave. He never let any barrier hold him back. "Fear is an illusion. Walk straight ahead, no matter what." That was one of his spiritual teachings that he said we would need, all the way to the very end. He taught us, "At the very final moment, walk through the fear and give yourself to God." Love is more powerful than fear, and I think Dave broke through all those barriers out of an intense love for God and for mankind.

He was not afraid of things that most people are afraid of. Let's take skunks, for example! At the ranch, we are out of the city limits, in a rural area, and so a lot of wild animals come through the property, including skunks. We had a dog, so it was not workable to have the skunks coming and going. We used a Havahart® trap, which does not harm the animals. We'd put peanut butter in the trap so that the skunk would eat it at night and be there in the morning. Dave would go out and send the little skunk lots of love. He'd drape a sheet over the top of trap, so the skunk wouldn't get startled. And somehow Dave was able to do all that without the skunk spraying! He'd lift the trap up, put it in the truck, and then take the skunk out to another little happy place about a mile away. He'd very carefully open up the trap, and the skunk was sometimes not even awake in there, and so Dave would scoot it out of the trap with his hands, just to get it to leave. And all this time, he said he was loving the skunk. They never sprayed him. I don't know too many people that would handle a skunk like that. He said, "I send them all the love I can." Some years, we had to take out 12 skunks in the spring and 12 in the fall.

Dave was extraordinary in his love of nature. He would look up at the clouds in the sky and say, "Aren't they beautiful today?" Most of us never think to look up; we're so wrapped up in our worries and thoughts. Or he would look at a little squirrel up in the tree throwing juniper berries down on the ground, and he'd say, "Isn't that cute?" I might be saying, "Oh, those squirrels! They're eating up all our fruit!" He'd say, "We'll grow more fruit. Half of it is for the animals, and half of it is for us." He just had this attitude that Nature is Godly, and that includes the trees, the grass, the animals, the sky, the garden, and all that lives.

He loved gardening. We planted every year and loved to see things grow—tomatoes, squash, fruit trees, etc. His favorite were the home-grown tomatoes. He taught me that you can always learn a lot from nature, because it's our own human nature. Life is life. For example, he liked to point out that in the forest, there are trees of all sizes and shapes; some are bent and some are straight, and there's nothing wrong with the bent trees. We don't have to "fix" them or wish they were different from what they are.

He loved the trees so much that he wouldn't let me cut a limb from a tree if it was growing against the side of the house. When we did construction, we had to build around the trees. That's why we have a tree growing in the middle of a room in our house. It goes straight up through the roof!

Another extraordinary thing about Dave is that he began writing his books and teaching in the last years of his life. Most people, when they reach their late sixties, seventies, and eighties, say, "Okay, now I get to retire and do what *I* want!" They look back on all their accomplishments and rest on their laurels. They spend their last couple of decades focused on the personal happiness of their own family, travel, and hobbies.

Not David. It's like he lived many lifetimes in one. First, he was a renowned psychiatrist, invited into the elite clubs of high society, and even knighted by the Prince of Denmark for his contributions to humanity. Then he left that whole outer life and went into seclusion for many years, in his "monastery of one," to give full attention to his inner states, healing, and the nature of consciousness. He was charting the Map of Consciousness®. He experienced the depths of hell, and all the way to the divine states at the top.

Who else could create a Map like that, unless they had experienced the whole terrain?

When the world needed him, he came back. He said, "I could have left the world and never come back, but I knew I had to stay and teach." And he started doing that in his late 60s and continued until he finally got to leave the world at 85! It was love that made it possible. He loved sharing. And he loved that everybody loved the work. He saw the impact of the work on people's lives. Nothing made him happier than to know he was helping others.

I think he knew that, when we started teaching, he only had a decade or so to teach. It was very important to him, to put down all the teachings that he could, to give people what they needed. His whole life was dedicated to helping mankind, and I don't know too many people who have done that as selflessly as he did.

I saw his extraordinary selflessness on a daily basis. He *lived* the work. He *was* the teachings. Every day, he did the work out of his inspiration to leave a complete body of material that anyone could go to, whoever was interested in living a spiritual life and, ultimately, surrendering one's life entirely to God.

Spiritual life, I will say, is not for everybody. When you're first starting out in spiritual life, you think it's all halos and roses, but it is actually very difficult. The farther you get into it, the more you have to give up of yourself and, in the end, your life is not your own. As Dave said often: "Straight is the path, and narrow is the way. Waste no time!"

When he began writing and speaking late in life, people saw the end result of his lifelong commitment to spiritual life. He had spent many years as a hermit, barely eating and having no money. He was totally in the hands of the Divine, and he had all that he needed. He said that someone would come up to him and say, "Hey, we'll take you out to lunch." Or a box of apples would appear on his doorstep, and then he'd have enough to eat for a week.

I would call Dave this: a saint among us. He referred to himself as a "sharer" or "teacher." He devoted his life to the enlightenment of mankind, and he was without any order, lineage, or institution to back him. He had no priesthood, ministry, or ashram. He stood alone as a teacher, sharing from his own experience and not anything else. He did not repeat what he heard from others. His life was his message. It came from inside of him.

Ordinary Man

He was extraordinary but he strove to be ordinary. The simplest things made him happy. He did not need or want "the latest" or the "newest" this or that. He had his favorite chair to sit in, where he could prop his feet up on a little table and watch the news. He had his favorite china cup for drinking espresso. He was happy wearing his favorite old corduroys. He looked forward to Friday Fish Night with our two friends who came over to share a home-cooked meal.

He said one time, "All a person really needs, is to feel loved and cared for, and I certainly have that!" He was happy with what he had. He didn't need "more." He didn't care about appearances because he knew *who* and *what* he was. He lived in a state of contentment.

Dave was a simple man, and he appreciated simple things. He could tell when things came from the heart, and that's what made him happy. It might be something simple, like somebody bringing homemade cookies. He liked a good home-cooked meal. We were both from the Midwest, so of course we grew up on meat and potatoes. He was conscious about organic vegetables, and we ate in a healthy way, but he also enjoyed a good steak once in a while and he loved it when I made meatloaf. He even wanted a hot dog on occasion. His attitude toward the pleasures in life was "everything in moderation" and then you're okay. He was non-attached.

At times, he had a hard time with the mundane things like feeding and taking care of his body. As I said earlier, he was not always in his body like you and me are. He didn't see his body as "me." In old age, he didn't like the time that had to be spent taking care of the body. He wanted to go within and tend to the soul.

For example, one time, he got dehydrated and almost didn't pull through. I realized he had been drinking nonstop espresso and no water! So, I had to make sure he drank a certain number of glasses of water every day. I had to stay on him about that, and he did it. He was willing to care for the body because he knew he still had more work to do, and it was the physical body that allowed him to communicate and share his love and wisdom with people in this earthly domain.

One of the reasons that my relationship with Dave worked is because I handled the linear details. We had to keep it simple for him because of the state he was in. In other words, I took care of the shopping, travel plans, event logistics, contracts, bills, computers, house maintenance, and other details. We were running Veritas Publishing, which he established to publish his books and lectures, and that took a lot of work! He needed someone to do the outer world work, so that he could concentrate on creating the body of teachings that he wanted to share. He had to have time and focus for that to emerge out of him.

As he aged, I also had to take care of his body. He did everything he could to help me with practical things, like taking care of the animals, but the reality was that his age and his inner state made it hard for him to do a lot of the practical things in the world and around the house.

One thing he was able to do almost every day until the end was to go out to the chicken house and gather the eggs. The eggs had to be collected every afternoon. It brought a smile to my face whenever I saw him and our dog, Kelsey, jump into the golf cart and go over to the chicken house and get the eggs. Kelsey knew when it was 3 p.m. and she'd jump up on her seat in the cart just as soon as she saw him in his cowboy hat with the egg basket in his hand. It was a simple thing, but it brought so much joy to both of them. He loved having the dog in the cart with him. It was just adorable. It was so ordinary—a man and his dog—but it brought so much joy.

Having a dog extends human life. That was one of the findings of our research. It's about the love. Dave told us in a lecture

(August 2002) that's why people give pets to their children, because the lovingness of the doggie's wagging tail and the kitty's purr, help the children "grasp their own capacity of lovingness." If you've ever seen a puppy with a child, it's a total love fest. The puppy's tail doesn't stop wagging, and the child doesn't stop giggling. It's like the dog helps us feel our own lovingness, and that lovingness extends our life.

If you look at how Dave teaches, it's common sense with a lot of spiritual application in it. He had a special gift to take the ordinary things of life, like a pet dog, and give them profound spiritual significance.

Right when our life got so busy with traveling and lectures, Dave said that he wanted a dog. I told him I didn't think I could handle another animal. We had three cats, thirty chickens, several ducks, and a high-maintenance African Grey parrot. Still, he really wanted a dog. Maybe he thought a dog would help him stay in the world.

So, we went to the Humane Society to adopt a dog. I told Dave when we walked in, "I don't want a dog with dark hair—all the hair will show everywhere." You can already guess what happened. There was this poor dark-haired dog sitting in the corner of the cage, looking forlorn. She was a large dog, real quiet and looking sad. I wasn't sure about her. Then Dave said, "I want that one." And we got Kelsey. She was part Border Collie, and she was already trained. She turned out to be a marvelous dog. Dave knew his animals. When he picked one out, it was the best animal that anyone could ever pick. I don't know how he did it. He could see the essence of a being. That is a characteristic that goes along with a spiritual teacher. They see that aura or essence in a being.

This is how Dave lived his ordinary life. He saw the Divine in everything. One of his teachings is: "The commonplace and God are not distinct." If we all just contemplated that sentence every day, greater love would be revealed to us.

Questions and Answers

Q: What was Doc's background and spiritual upbringing?
A: He was raised in the Episcopal church, and he maintained his membership in that church throughout his life. He said his family was "high church" Episcopalian. He talks about it in some of the lectures. As a boy, he was an acolyte and he sang in the boys' choir. He talks about how he was "scrupulous" about every little "sin," and so he made sure he went to confession before partaking in the mass, so that he didn't have any "spot" on his soul! Even as a youngster, Dave took the spiritual realm seriously.

We each have whatever religion or faith that we were raised in, and so did he. But he realized that there are other religions that have the same basic quest, the same basic goals: to believe there is a higher being and to become a better person.

David was unique because he studied and experienced all the different religions. He read everything, and he tried everything. Buddhism, Hinduism, Sufism, and more. He was an atheist for a while, then agnostic. He tried the science route. He explored every possible path to Truth. He wanted to understand why the different religions did what they did, such as the Sufis that dance and dance and dance.

He didn't just read books, however. In fact, he talks about how he gave away all his books at one point. He *experienced* all the different paths. In his books and lectures, he talks about some of his other lifetimes as a Buddhist and Hindu. And in this lifetime, he experienced different religious paths.

The body of work that Dave created came out of his own inner experience. When I joined him, we were able to do the research together, thousands of calibrations so that people would have what they needed to discern the truth. He was in a class by himself. When he wrote the book, *Truth versus Falsehood*, it's like he knew what was going to happen in the world, 15-20 years before it happened. He was way ahead of his time as to the political climate and the global issues. It is amazing to me that he could see into the future like that.

David was an exceptional person. He coined words like "integrous." He coined phrases like "devotional nonduality" and "Homo spiritus." My personal favorite is "hermeneutics of epistemology"—that one really throws people for a loop!

Q: Doc did a lot of dancing. Was that something that you saw him use as a spiritual practice?

A: No, it was just an enjoyment for him. He said that he understood how the Sufi Whirling Dervishes could do that. He would begin to dance, and soon the dance would be dancing him for many hours. He said that you get into a high state like the Sufi dancers do, except they are doing it as a religious ritual, which is different from doing it because you enjoy it. Many years ago, there was a Franciscan monastery that had a little chapel which was open all night, and Dave said he would dance in there, alone, through the night.

Q: Are there any things that Doc taught, but that people often overlook?

A: You know how hard it is just to be kind to everyone?! That was one of Dave's teachings to us. "Be kind to everything and everyone, without exception, no matter what, including yourself." Actually, he said that if we just focus on this single tool, of kindness, it will take us the whole way. But it's not easy to do! For example: someone is nasty to you at the checkout stand, and then you have to turn around and say in a kind way, "You're not having a good day, are you?" That happened to me recently, and I remembered what Dave taught me: "You don't know what's happening in their lives, so give them the benefit of the doubt. They might have just gotten bad news. Their dog might have just died!" And, so, we can't hold it against them because they're probably not normally like that. We all have our down moments. When you're in the public and you're working with people, it's hard to remain that steady person. We have to show mercy to people.

Q: Was there anything about Doc's career as a psychiatrist that surprised you?

A: Yes, when he told me about going to Woodstock! It was the huge famous musical concert in the summer of 1969. Half a million or more people flooded into a little dairy farm in New York. Dave went there to treat people who were having bad trips on LSD. He was a psychiatrist working on a unit that was treating people for the bad trips they were having on various drugs, and some of them didn't even know what they had taken. He said that Woodstock was a great time. He got to see terrific musicians like Janis Joplin. It was wild because of all the traffic and the electrical shortages on stage. At some point, a truckload of watermelon came into the camp, and everybody was eating watermelon, spitting the seeds all over the ground. It rained and rained and was a muddy mess. He said, "I wanted to go back to that field the next year and see how many watermelons came up!" I think he was really happy he got to go there and help people.

Dave helped a lot of people as a physician. He had the largest psychiatric practice in New York, maybe even the country, because so many people came to him for help. He told me once that, as a physician, he could only help one person at a time, but he could help more people if he wrote books and gave lectures. So, we decided that he would start to lecture so that he could reach more people.

Q: We're a Hawkins Study Group that has been meeting for many years. We're very grateful for Doc and you. Your work has totally transformed our lives!

A: It's beautiful to be able to move people's lives in the right direction, like Dave was able to do. I am grateful to all the lives that he changed and all the people that understand the work. I want to thank each and every one of you, because your commitment helps me to continue with the work. It gives me incentive to keep going. Maybe we can reach more people who are out there waiting for this kind of teaching to help them with their lives. Some of the people that Doc helped didn't even believe in God or any kind of Higher Being. But when they read a book or heard him, that's when their heart turned toward a higher purpose. And that, in itself, is a testimony that there is a Divine Presence that is helping us through our everyday lives, and so we need to call on that Presence when we are in dire straits. When we cry out, the Presence is there. It's always there. I don't care what you call "It," but that Higher Power or Presence is always there when you really need it. And it may come in a form that you don't expect. Sometimes the worst things that happen to us are the very things that wake us up.

As an individual, each person has to understand that they have—if they're at all interested in the spiritual side—a certain light within their aura. And it's just a matter of turning on the light in a dark room to pursue this, and to improve yourself as a human being, and in return, you actually become a channel of that light in the world. But you have to be willing to do the work and to give it from your heart.

Life is filled with so many different things. You have your love-mate and family. There's your work, there's raising children, there are your animals, there's growing your garden, there's music and other artistic endeavors, there are all kinds of things that are a part of your life. By becoming one with the world through these various ordinary endeavors, you realize you are a part of this whole big picture of life. Some people, like Dave, are meant to change it in a big way. And most of us are meant to change it in a smaller way. But 'big and small' doesn't matter except to the ego. If our heart is in the right place, then we're all changing the world for the better. The power to do that is inside all of us. Dave's work lights that spark of the Holy Spirit in our soul.

Dave used the wonderful example of the ships on the sea. You can't lift the ships on the sea one by one, but you can lift the ocean and then all the ships automatically are lifted. So, if you improve yourself, then you raise the water level for everyone. You raise your own level of consciousness and then the consciousness of the world is automatically raised, and all the ships are raised.

Dave worked hard to raise the level of the whole sea. To put another way, he raised the water level so that the mountains we had to climb were shorter!

He gave his life to helping others. He worked nonstop in his last years of life to leave us this complete body of work in both lectures and books, because he wanted everyone to have the opportunity to become a better person, spiritually. I'm thankful that he was here on earth for the time that he was, and I'm grateful to have spent a part of it with him, in the background of it all. I'm happy to know that I helped him achieve his goals, which was to explain to people about healing and spirituality—that we have to nourish our soul. And it doesn't require a structured religion to do this, though sometimes religion can help because of the uplifting messages and the feeling of camaraderie.

Q: What's the most important thing for us to know on the spiritual path?
A: Humility. Dave said that humility is the "most powerful tool to move up in levels of consciousness (Power vs Force video)." And I agree with him on that. He lived it. Like I've said, he was an exceptional, extraordinary person, but he was totally humble. He didn't see himself as better than anyone else. He taught me that you have to be humble enough to ask for help from the Holy Spirit, or whoever your Higher Being is. He said, "No one is able to move up the levels of consciousness unaided." We depend on Grace, and without humility, we would not see our need for it. We would think, "Oh look how far I've come!" With humility, we realize we are where we are because of Grace. Something or Someone allowed us to be where we are. Dave said that humility is the "cornerstone" of our spiritual life.

Q: It's a blessing to serve a realized Master, and every moment is a learning when you live with him. I would like to hear how *you* felt when you were serving him and how your life with him was like a learning.

A: I learned a lot about mankind and the upside and the downside of mankind. We have both of those. No matter who we are, we all have our upside and downside. And he approached the downside with humor. He taught me through humor. He would laugh about things that other people went on and on crying about, because he saw the innocence of the insanity of it all. So much of what happens in the world is ironic, so he would make it into a joke. He would laugh about it and say, "Can you believe that?!" Looking at mankind, he taught me how to approach the most awful things in mankind, as well as the most radiant aspects of spiritual life. It was on a daily basis. Things would happen and he was accepting of everything. He was very accepting of humankind. He embraced every facet. Now, for me, it's difficult to embrace certain things, but through his eyes, I was able to do that. And through his eyes, I learned to not take everything so seriously. There's always a humorous side to it, and from that point of view, you can cope with the downside of mankind.

Q: What was Doc's guidance on peace and joy?

A: You can see his face light up when you talk about peace and joy. It's like it's just a radiance that someone has, and you know it comes from within. You know it when you're around it. It's not what they say but what they are, when you know that person is coming from the heart. We have a friend who does it in her writing. She comes from the heart and has a way of putting that into words. Dave came from the heart in everything he did. He loved his fellow man, and he wanted to make their burdens easier. That's how we spread peace and joy—through our own inner happiness and joy, and then it spills out to everyone we meet. I think if we could all do that a little bit, each in our own way, that's how we will add something positive to the world. Dave taught us that if we understand the essence of any single thing, then we know God. So, we don't have to know everything, we just have to truly love the essence of one thing.

PART III:
ON THE ROAD WITH DOC

7

ON STAGE

Dave was magnetic when he spoke. From where I sat on stage, I could see everyone in the audience and how they were transformed as he spoke. One moment they were laughing and, in the next, they were weeping. The seminars were electrifying because of the energy. He and I were giving everything of ourselves to all the people, and they were giving all their love back to us.

Someone asked me recently about "the silent transmission." When Dave walked out onto the stage, that higher consciousness came through him. And what came back at us, standing there, was an audience of hundreds of people looking at us with boundless love. You cannot imagine how powerful that was. The transmission of love that they gave us almost knocked me over when I first experienced it. They were all sending us the vibration of the soul. It was their internal interpretation of what they were going to experience that day. The inner Self is very powerful.

The Self spoke through David to the Self of the listeners. He would pick out a lecture topic ahead of time, but he didn't know what he would say until the words came out of his mouth. He said, "I'm hearing it for the first time myself, as I'm speaking it to you. The group here brings out what needs to be said today." He was a conduit of higher teaching. Through him, the Self transmitted what everybody needed to get from that lecture. From where I sat, I could see that he reached every person in the audience at one time or another. When it was over, people did not want to leave. They were engulfed in the love.

What people didn't know is that, backstage, before the lecture, Dave would have a sort of meltdown. He'd look at me and say, "I don't think I can do this. I just don't think I can go out there and do this lecture." The volunteers standing with us would get worried: "What are we going to do with this room full of people?" I would tell him, "Oh, yes, Dave, you can do this." He would pray, and he would surrender. He would invoke Jesus Christ just like you might invoke Buddha or whatever Deity or religion is yours. You invoke them to help you and to guide you. Dave would do that and then he'd totally surrender and go out there on stage. And, then, Wow! It was like the Holy Spirit came right through him!

The way that he presented his material gave us an *experience* of it. The transmission of that higher consciousness came *through* him and then we could understand it. And so consequently, we say, "Doc said this," but I think it was the transmission from a higher place. He had become one with that higher plane. That's who and what he was. We all put him up on a pedestal, because we're not able to communicate in that way, and we don't have the same knowledge that he had, but it wasn't a personal self that spoke to us.

When I was on stage with him, I saw how Divine Grace came through him and he would say things in a powerful way and suddenly people's faces would light up—they got it! It was so fulfilling to see that response and to know that someone's life was changed. For Dave, it was never about *him*. He only cared about the message and its impact on others. He had an infectious sense of humor; it was impossible not to laugh whenever he was laughing. He didn't care about appearances or getting approval from others, because he was at peace with himself and his efforts.

He gave a hundred different lectures all over the world. We video-recorded all of them, and they are available through our website, currently in a streaming service. Here I'd like to share with you just a few of the highlights from my experience.

The Lecture Begins

As people arrived inside the event room, they would hear a beautiful chant called "Kyrie Eleison," by Robert Gass & On Wings of Song (Springhill Media). This music calibrates in the 700s. Dave liked using it at the lectures because it set the tone for the day by giving people an experience of that Divine state. We played "Kyrie" on the speakers for the whole hour leading up to the lecture, as people mingled and meditated, and then at the end of the lecture, when Dave gave a final blessing, we played "Alleluia," another chant from the same album.

When it was time for the lecture to begin, Dave would come out on stage with something to make people laugh—a rubber chicken, a funny hat, a puppet, or a funny joke. For example, here's a joke he told at a lecture at the Institute of Noetic Sciences (2003):

> We thought of a funny joke this morning. What is a New Ager? Somebody who goes to the store and buys all the Venus Fly Traps and wants them to become vegetarians! *Laughter*... Oh, yeah sure, just take away the fly that it wants to eat! "You like cucumbers, sweetheart, remember?! Here's a piece of tomato, don't you like it?" *Laughter*... We have to laugh at our own naiveté. The spiritual child within us believes in Santa Claus and all kinds of wonderful things, and it's painful as we grow up into spiritual maturity.

When he was getting older, he'd use his cane to start off the lecture in a comical way. One time, he came out from behind the curtain and acted like he could barely walk. He was so dramatic, limping and hunching over, dragging his feet, making a long, drawn face. Then suddenly, he turned into Fred Astaire for a moment, doing a little tap dance across the stage with his cane. He laughed and said, "Yep, so you see? Part of being an old man is having a cane. It's part of the whole scene. You can't be an old man unless you have a cane!"

After he got everyone to laugh over something funny, he had three things that he liked to say at the start of his lectures. First, he always began with: *Gloria in Excelsis Deo*—"Glory to God in the Highest." Then he would make a joke by saying something like, "If you have a problem with that, you can leave now before we get started. You'll save yourself the headache of hearing something you don't like!"

Second, he liked to say: "Nothing causes anything. Everything arises spontaneously of its own, by virtue of what it is." Of course, nobody knew what he meant by this, but he figured if he repeated it enough then maybe one day, a light would go off. He was trying to take us beyond the mind, beyond causality. Everyone's mind is linear and assumes that something *causes* something else.

One time, in front of a very scientific audience, he started off with, "Well, today we're going to transcend the mind because it's a big nuisance!" They didn't understand what he meant, but they laughed because he was laughing. He was a genius speaking in front of a very intelligent and sophisticated audience, and he was saying that the mind is a nuisance! He used humor to get people on board with him into a space beyond the mind and its resistance to new ideas. When you're laughing, you are very open.

Third, he told us at the beginning of a lecture why we were there: "The only reason people are here today is because they're destined for enlightenment." I remember one woman came all the way from South Korea to attend a lecture and she couldn't understand a word in English! She asked, "Why am I here?" Maybe a lot of people wondered that same question.

The only reason people are here today is because they're destined for enlightenment. Nobody else would be here! In the Newtonian paradigm, you think you're the product of your past. You think you're here because the past has pushed you here. That's old fashioned—forget it! *Laughter...* In the new paradigm, which is also describable in quantum mechanics, it's the future that's pulling you to be where you are.... Your future is why you're here. If you weren't destined to be enlightened, no-body would be here. If you weren't interested in playing golf, you wouldn't be taking golf classes, right? *Laughter...* Let's see if what we said is so. *Arm test with Susan.* What I just said is a fact. *Muscle test – yes.* They are all destined for enlightenment. *Yes.* Who else but people destined for enlightenment would be at a class on how to become enlightened? It's rather obvious, isn't it?

So, in those first few minutes, he had covered pretty much ev-erything we needed to know. He would say, "We like to start at the end. That way, you can leave now and not miss much!" Of course, no one left. They were all glued to their seats, and when it was over, we had to *make* people leave!

Fun Topics

Dave was always creating new words and phrases. One of the fun-niest things that ever happened to us on stage was when he said "hermeneutics of epistemology" at a lecture where a woman was signing for the deaf. You should have seen the look on her face—she just froze! She couldn't figure out how to sign it. Her little hands had been working like mad during the lecture, trying to keep up with him. And then when he said, "hermeneutics of epistemol-ogy," she just put her hands together and held them still. What else could she do?! There was nothing that she could figure out to sign, unless she spelled it out, and how would you do that on the spot? The look on her face was priceless. I'll never forget it.

Dave loved the animal kingdom. Every creature fascinated him. The Komodo dragon was one of his favorite animals to talk about in lectures. He said it was a living example of the dinosaur era. He understood it. He didn't judge it. The Komodo dragon has an en-ergy that calibrates at 70, which is deadly, but Dave explained it in a way that was so animated, he had us laughing. "Its only intention is ME, ME, ME, and in order for ME to survive, it's necessary to kill and eat YOU. The Komodo dragon has perfected that." And then Dave would act out what the Komodo dragon does. He would pantomime it. "One bite and—it doesn't even have to kill you—it just has to bite you and then it settles down and waits until you die, so it can have its dinner!" And he'd lick his lips and pat his stomach like you do after a delicious dinner. "As you can see, its intention is not spiritually corrupt. It's not intending to kill you, it just intends to have dinner! The tiger doesn't kill the rabbit. He just has lunch. Yummmmm! That's warm, four-legged lunch! The tiger likes warm lunch and has a propensity for rabbits!"

By getting us to laugh at the animal, he was getting us to accept the nature of the ego. It isn't evil. It just wants to survive, and it will steal and kill in order to do so! After hearing Dave talk about this so many times, it hit home with me. Whenever I go out to my garden in the mornings and see that javelina and rabbits have eaten all my kale, I think about what he said. Just when the greens are ready to pick and eat, I go out there to get some, and they're all gone! The animals aren't being mean; they're just eating their dinner! When I see it that way, then it's easy to let it go. Dave taught me how to make peace with the animals; they are just doing what they do. And same with the "animal" inside of human beings!

What I learned from Dave is that we all have a little Komodo dragon in us. It's the reptile in our unconscious, Dave would say. One of our jokes at home was, "If you're gonna rattle my cage, make sure it's locked!"

At his lecture at the Institute for Noetic Sciences in 2003, Dave talked about how all these energies are in our unconscious. He said: "I had Freudian analysis for many years.... When you begin to look into the unconscious, you go into shock because what you're going to discover there is what you see in the reptile, the animal ... the 'me-me' self-centeredness."

And that, he said, is the ego. "The ego is what's left of the animal still in us." One time, he came out on stage with a little stuffed brown teddy bear. It was so cute, with a little red ribbon around its neck. He held it up close, sort of hugging it, and said, "This is our little ego. See how adorable he is? He's not 'evil', is he? No! He's just self-centered. He's like your little pet. He wants what he wants. You don't have to hate your little pet ego, see?" And then he hugged it and patted it on the head and said, "There, there, little pet ego, I know you want to kill the guy that cut you off in traffic! He deserves to die, doesn't he?" Of course, the room was roaring with laughter.

Then he'd go into his charts on the screen, showing how this little "ego" had evolved over the millennia. By the time he finished, you actually felt grateful for the thing! Look how hard it has worked to get us to where we are today. Thanks to the ego for being so self-centered in its quest to survive! "Otherwise, we wouldn't be sitting here today," Dave would say. So, the point isn't to hate the ego but to transcend it. In one lecture (Institute for Noetic Sciences, 2003), Dave told the audience:

> Life evolves from self-centeredness. It's not spiritually corrupt because it's just being what it is. Life evolves from self-centeredness and survival. It then evolves to higher forms. In the mother bird for the first time, we see caring about another. The reptile doesn't care about another. It lays its eggs and wanders away. But in the mother bird, there is concern about the eggs and the little baby birds … and then with the evolution of mammalian life, we see the first appearance of real concern for others and the first appearance of love. Love arises, presents itself, through the maternal, through the feminine, which begins to express concern, caringness, etc.

> For those doing spiritual work and especially those interested in transcending the ego, we give the outlines of the intrinsic structure of the ego. To approach the ego, then, it's necessary to hold it in a certain contextual manner so as not to go into guilt, self-flagellation, and suicide. *Laughter…*

So, Dave had a way of helping us laugh at our ego. It's a pet. We can treat it like we do our pets at home. We just have to keep it out of trouble and, of course, give it a treat every once in a while. Even Dave liked to have his ice cream after dinner!

That reminds me of another saying that Dave liked to say, "Just because you love vanilla doesn't mean you have to hate chocolate." It was his way of referencing the politics of our time, how people take a stand for one side of an issue and then think they have to hate the other side. Since his passing, the divisiveness has only gotten worse! The ego is into good and bad, us versus them. That's what we have to watch out for. When he put it in terms of flavors, chocolate and vanilla, it's obvious. You can have a preference for one flavor without hating the other.

"Well, I don't know if we're going to transcend the ego before we take our lunch break, or after!" When he said that at a lecture, everyone laughed. "But, don't worry, we'll give you a hint: The ego deals in dualities—good and bad, etc... so watch out if you get into goodness and badness. The mind becomes dualistic."

So, the ego deals with dualities and that's what he wanted us to get beyond. It's very hard to do that! I face that challenge every day.

Recently, I was dealing with the fires here in Arizona. The little town where Dave and I have a cabin—where he wrote a lot of his books, and where some of my family lives—was evacuated. I was told that our cabin might burn down because it backs up to a forest area. That sounds bad, doesn't it? And it *is* bad, when you first look at it, but I was also looking at it from the other side. Because of the fires, we are appreciating and respecting Mother Nature more. Our hearts go out to the wild animals who are being displaced. Someone sent me a video of elk running out of the forest. Our hearts open up when we see that. We're also appreciating the fire fighters more. They risk their lives to fight these fires for weeks, sometimes months. It's just amazing what they can do. It's a dangerous occupation, especially with the heat. We're all praying more. We're praying for rain and for the people and for the animals.

And just when I was getting adjusted to that fire, another fire broke out closer to home in Sedona. I was wondering, *Will I have to evacuate? What will I do with all the animals, with the computers, with all of Dave's things here?* I knew that if it happened, I would handle it in some way, but I would also have to let go of some things because you can't take everything with you when you evacuate. I have 30 chickens, and there would be no way to evacuate them. You feel sad to think what would happen. But then I imagine what Dave would say, and it would be, "Well, I guess we're going to have some fried chicken!" As you can see, he was not into sentimentalism!

So, life is always changing, and we have to adapt. Dave wanted us to get beyond the duality of, "This is good, this is bad." Most people are stuck in that positionality. From my perspective, I am always trying to figure out the lesson. I think that all of us have lessons to learn, especially if we are facing a crisis. There was a lesson for me, with these fires.

Maybe it was to see the importance of basic kindness. My sister was taking care of my brother in hospice at her home. That was hard enough. And then the fire came, and people were getting evacuated. One night, her husband came home from work and there were several people crashed on his porch in sleeping bags. He said, "Who are these people? I don't even know them." My sister had opened up her house to them. No matter what you're going through, there's always room for kindness, caring, and compassion.

A lot of Dave's insights like this went into me while I was on stage listening to him. And now, since his passing, I try to apply those insights to everyday life. That's really where the work is. Each moment we have a choice to heed the lesson or ignore it. Like he said, we are just little iron filings, being pulled toward the magnet according to our destiny and our free-will choices. When we make one decision, our "charge" goes one way, and when we make another decision, our "charge" goes the other way. It's either positive or negative. We're all these little iron filings trying to do the right thing so that we eventually reach the "top of the Map," so to say. Whether we do it in this lifetime or not, that is up to us, our ability, how much time we devote to our Higher Self, and of course, everything depends upon karma and God's will.

To meet a good and true teacher like David is a great blessing. And, then, to actually apply his teachings in our daily life, and with everyone we meet—that's the hard part and also the most fulfilling part!

Dave always wanted us to be forgiving of ourselves and others. He had a lot of compassion for humankind. He made a joke about it one time in a lecture:

> We are in the difficult position of being human beings. I feel compassionate toward all human beings. If I were St. Peter, I'd let everybody in.
>
> I'd say, "Where ya been?"
>
> "Earth."
>
> "Okay, You're in!" *Laughter...*
>
> So, you realize the strength, courage, and valor that it takes to lead a human life. If you're honest with yourself about your own life and realize that everybody has lived that and then some, you respect all of life.

Dave said he'd even have compassion for the guy at the gallows who had to chop his head off: "The headsman, as he chops off my head, I pray he doesn't feel bad about it. I tell him, 'Look, man, it's only your job. Just do a good job, nice and quick.'" Dave's gallows humor was very cathartic for people.

Serious Moments

One of the most unique lectures we did was during the Harmonic Concordance, when all the planets lined up in November, 2003. It was an event for the Learning Annex in San Francisco. The energy in that room was tremendous. There were about four hundred people there—a very spiritually committed group. At a certain point in the lecture, just when the Harmonic Concordance was occurring, we stopped and everyone prayed or meditated silently for those ten minutes, and then we did an "Om." All over the world, spiritually committed people were praying and meditating for those ten minutes, and we joined them. The energy in the room was intensely powerful.

Dave and I calibrated that the consciousness level of mankind jumped from 205 to 207 during that ten minutes. It was an amazing experience. It's not anything that you can put into words, but you realize you are not the same afterwards. You realize that human devotion and prayer, if it's put to that selfless intention, can impact the entire collective consciousness of mankind.

We stayed at this huge hotel, right in San Francisco. It was beautiful. We could see the Bay Bridge out of the window. The hotel was so big that David could hardly walk to our room. Here was Dave, in his little body that could barely walk to our hotel room, yet the energy was so powerful when he was on stage. It's like with Mother Teresa. Big energy can come from small things.

When I was on stage with Dave, he was always surprising me. I sat through every lecture and every Satsang. I thought I knew how he would explain something. I'd be sitting there, thinking, *Oh, okay, he's going to say this again.* Then, all of a sudden, he said it in a slightly different way, and BOOM! I got it. The light went on. And I would think, *Oh, my! So THAT's what it means!* This happened to me many times. It's like it finally goes into your being. Maybe you heard many times before, but now it becomes a part of who you are. He had a way of repeating things over and over but from a slightly different angle, and then finally you "got" it, because he had shown it to you from every angle.

Sometimes he surprised me in how he answered people's questions. I might be sitting up there and smugly thinking, *I know how he's gonna answer this person.* And, then, what he said was very different than what I thought he was going to say, and I would be floored. Sometimes, when I thought he was going to give someone the "Zen whack," he would be so gentle with them. It was amazing to me how he sensed exactly how to answer every person who came on stage to bare their soul to him.

The time that shocked me the most was at one of our last lectures. I thought, *Whoa, I never saw that one coming!* A woman came up on stage to ask Dave a question. She said she had been molested when she was young. Whenever I hear that, it's always a heavy load for me to carry. Then, she asked something like, "How do I live with this? How do I forgive this person?" I was expecting Dave to be sweet with her, but he gave her a Zen whack. That's what I call it when he came down hard on people, to help them let go of negative baggage.

Dave said to her, "How long ago did this happen?" She said, "Forty years." He said, "Well then why are you still carrying it?" There was a stunned silence. And I thought, *Yeah, why is she?*

He said to her, "Get over it! How long are you going to hang on to that? You're juicing it. You've been living with this for 40 years, and you're still carrying it around? You are not your past. That's not who you really are!"

He wanted her to move on and become the person she was supposed to become, and not identify as a victim who had been molested when she was young. She was not that child any longer. Dave wanted to free her of that baggage.

At first, I was shocked that he said that to her. I was not expecting the Zen whack. But then, sitting there, I realized, *Yeah, he's right, she has to let that go.* Bad things happen to good people all the time. If we take the responsibility for our own lives, then we can move forward, but we have to let go of juicing being the victim of something. Dave helped a lot of people that way, and their lives were changed. In that woman's case, Dave gave her the Zen whack and it was his "tough love" as he called it.

He knew when he should be tough with people and when he should not be. He was very good at knowing what the soul of a person needed in a particular moment. It is a special person who can do that with someone's life and say, "Okay, it's time for you to get over that. Snap out of it!" I always think of the film *Moonstruck* when the character goes, "Snap out of it!" That's what Dave would do. I don't think anyone else could do it like he did it. He was a sage.

He answered each person in their soul. People asked some of the same questions over and over again, but he answered it differently each time. The question itself might be the same as what another person had asked, but he would answer it entirely differently because a different person was asking it he was speaking to that person's own inner self. Underneath the question they asked, he sensed their silent inner question. I don't know how he did that. And, also, he was answering them at the same time that he was sitting there signing stacks of books for people. He was extraordinary.

At the Satsangs, people would ask him questions and he knew exactly what they needed. There was one lady who had a lot of problems, mentally, and he was so kind to her because he understood her. He knew she couldn't do anything differently. He encouraged her to get back on her medication. He could tell that she needed it. She did that, and she got better. She was a sweet soul. He could sense when people needed help, when they needed tenderness, and when they needed the Zen whack.

He would look at you and read you and know what to say to you. He'd be there signing the books, and someone new would come up from the line and sit down with us on stage to ask their question. Dave would glance up to look at the person and then go back to his book-signing. From that one glance, he already knew what they were and what they needed. Often, he just looked in their eyes and that was it. And then he would go, "Well, you need to do this and this and this..." And off with you!

Dave was inspiring to me. So many people have told me, "Your husband is such an inspiration to me, and I understand the spiritual dimension of life because of him." He knew what to say to them about how to get better. What he said was not always sweet and rosy—sometimes it was that Zen whack! He knew when to pull that out and when not to; he knew when people needed encouragement and when they needed a challenge. I've heard so many testimonies from people whose lives were changed by listening to Dave at a lecture.

Most of the time, people were changed during the lecture, but we didn't know because they never told us. Here's a case that I heard about from one of our longtime students. He was at a lecture in Santa Monica, California, where many of the people in attendance had no clue as to what Dave was. They had signed up because it was in a paper that advertised consciousness events. Our lecture was listed right alongside an event that was something equivalent to a course on how to be a porn star! When it's their time, I guess people come in the door however they get there.

So, our student was telling me about sitting at a table during the lunch break, and he overheard two guys just railing on us, how ridiculous the lecture was, etc. They had no clue about Dave, and they thought the lecture was bad. But then, lo and behold, toward the end of the day, one of them went up on stage to ask Dave a question, and his demeanor was sincere and serious. He had been transformed. As our student put it, "Something happened to that guy! He was a different person from lunchtime!"

I told our student who had seen this, "You were gifted with seeing it. It's a lesson for *you*. We're so accustomed to hearing these things that we may not be aware when it's actually a lesson for *us*. So, we have to start looking more closely at, 'Now why would I see that?' Ask yourself, 'Why did I have to see that?' Because it's a teaching for *you*."

So sometimes the gift is being transformed, and sometimes the gift is witnessing the transformation of others.

Questions and Answers

Q: Did Doc ever struggle with doubt when he was challenged or criticized?
A: No. He made every effort to communicate clearly. But he didn't care what people thought. He would state things so bluntly

sometimes that I would cringe, yet he knew what people needed. He would repeat what Jesus said, "He who has ears, let him hear." If someone didn't like what Dave said, he surrendered them to God and to their own karma.

Q: Which intellectual minds was Doc most inspired by?
A: The *Great Books of the Western World*. Of course, he often mentioned Socrates, Jung, and Freud. He was a psychiatrist, and that gave him tools to examine different things, as he crossed over from psychiatry into the spiritual. He was unique in that he could see the inside track, into how the brain functions. To most of us, it's a tangled-up mess! I remember him looking to find the answers, and then figuring out how to present to people. When we were doing the chart on the consciousness levels of the animal kingdom, I remember how he worked hard to create a single chart that broke down the evolution of consciousness over eons of time. He was able to put millions of years of planetary evolution into one chart! Most of us can't even put one day's worth of emotion into one chart—we are all across the board!

Q: Did you and Doc know that you'd be traveling so much and giving lectures all over the place?
A: When we started, it was in Sedona, our hometown. He said, "I'm only going to do twelve lectures for a year, and only write three books." But once he got started in the lectures, they wouldn't let him stop. People all over the world started reading his books, and they sent requests for us to come there and speak.

Each lecture, he gave a lot of thought to it. He wanted to repeat certain basic information, and also bring in something new. He got to where he would pick out slides that he thought were important, and he would run through those basic ones, and then he would cover the slides that outlined the new material he had developed for that lecture. The *Book of Slides* has all the lecture slides and gives explanations. If you read through that book, you will understand what Dave presented.

In his presentations, he wanted to touch on the different types of people and how they learn. Some people get it through listening, some through visualizing, some through feeling. Those are the three key learning styles, so he presented his material in all three ways so that everyone would understand the work. That's why I think he reached so many of us, because everyone is different, and Dave's lectures encompassed all those dimensions.

Q: What was the purpose of muscle-testing on stage?
A: Dave and I used it because we did not want to say anything that was not true. Dave said he didn't want the karma of saying or writing something that wasn't true. So, by doing kinesiology, it was our way of testing to make sure that we were getting and giving the correct information. Everything that we've done or said or taught has all been tested. We'd say, "We think this is it, but let's test it." It was Dave's way of making sure that it was for the highest good that he said or wrote something.

Q: It seems so obvious when watching the videos over and over that Doc had no vested interest in the outcome of a test. He just wanted the truth.
A: Right. He wanted the truth. I noticed this the other day when I was watching a video of a lecture, that I always looked at Dave's eyes and then I shut my own eyes when he pushed down on my arm. I looked at his eyes, not at what he was doing, and then I closed my eyes. If I was looking at him while doing the arm, I don't think I would have gotten the correct answer, because of his energy. I'd just go strong all the time.

Q: Didn't Doc have other ways of knowing the same information? It seemed that he intuited the answer and then confirmed it with the arm.
A: A lot of times at the lectures he intuited and then he would check the arm to make sure. He always checked to make sure, in everything he said or wrote. And also, that way, it was a verification

for everyone present, to see it with their own eyes.

Q: Doc was never on stage without you. Why was that?
A: I don't know why. It was just the way it was. I was the arm, so I guess I had to be on stage!

Q: It seemed that you helped the communication between him and people who were asking him questions. He relied on your presence for something. It's like you helped to boil their verbiage down for him.
A: Yes, that's true. A lot of people didn't know how to ask a question of him. They would go up there and speak a lot of verbiage, trying to express themselves, saying this and this and this. In many cases, I think they were so flustered by being up there with Dave, that they couldn't remember their question. It was the energy of this person that you're sitting in front of, it overwhelms you, and you lose your train of thought. Dave would often get lost if people gave a lot of mental verbiage. He just needed the essence of it, so he'd ask me, "What did they say?" And I would boil it down to the simple essence, to what I knew he could register.

Q: And it seemed like sometimes you were a protector.
A: I had to be. There were people that came up with bad energies. You can get them right away, using a sixth sense. Still, a few people slipped through. Also, we had to protect Dave from people who wanted to catch him at the break time at lectures. He just needed downtime and they were coming to talk to him. We had to put up a sign to keep people out. Or they were hovering to grab his Diet Pepsi can. It was strange. They were like vultures hovering around, wanting to grab anything that he touched. There were the "takers" and the "givers." We tried to protect Dave from the "takers."

Q: Was the lecturing hard on Doc?
A: People didn't know what he suffered behind the scenes. At one point, his vertebrae had collapsed on his back. He had to wear

a vest that would hold his back straight, to keep his vertebrae in place. It was like a straight-jacket. That's when he had to stop giving hugs to people. In the early lectures, people would go up on stage to ask a question and they'd want a hug. He'd say, "For a dollar!" It became a great joke. But then when his back went out, he had to say, "No more hugs. My bones are like Styrofoam." He had so much pain, he could hardly get in and out of bed. And yet, for the love of the work, and for his students, he got up, and put on that vest, and went to do the lecture. His students never knew what he went through because he didn't mention it. He never complained. But I was aware of the pain he was going through in order to do the lecture. He knew that he had something that people needed to hear it, and he put his love out there for everyone who attended.

Q: What was it like after the lectures?
A: It took us a while to come down off that energy. We'd come home and neither one of us could calm down. It was a long day, driving there, setting up, teaching, talking to people at lunch, teaching more, driving home. By the end of the day, we were tired, but also wired! Sometimes we wouldn't get done until 10 or 11 at night, so we'd watch the news or whatever we could do to unwind. I'm really amazed when I think about the fact that we did this nonstop for ten years.

We did lectures for so many different places and people. We went to Toronto, New York, San Francisco, San Diego, Chicago, and so forth. It was very moving to know that committed people were coming in from all these different areas just to hear Dave speak. When people are interested in spirituality, they find their way to a teaching or a teacher. It's in their soul. That's been going on since the beginning of mankind.

One time I met a little lady when I was up in Canada. She came a long way to see us. It's really amazing how people will travel such distances for their spiritual faith, to receive the transmission of the teachings. When you're in that presence, you know it. That's why you travel any distance to encounter it.

Q: Doc was dynamic on stage. Was he different at home?

A: As a person to live with, he was very even, without ups and downs. Of course, I did hound him about his clothes! Because he didn't care what he looked like. He knew who he was. He knew he was a spiritual being. He was comfortable in his body. Speaking of being comfortable in his body, he told me a story of when he was in the Navy, living in San Francisco as a young man. He was walking along, and this lady approached him, and she said, "Would you like to make 50 bucks?" He said, "What do I have to do?" She replied, "I need you as a nude model for an art class." He wanted the money and so he said, "Sure I'll do that!"

People were always drawn to him. It had nothing to do with the physical body. It's true for us too. It's your soul that people read. They look at you and they connect with the spirit. The only thing we take to the next life is our soul. So what are we going to do to improve our connection with it? It's up to us to make that decision on what we will do to nourish our soul so that when we pass over, we don't have any regrets.

8

STORIES AND EXPERIENCES

"As a doctor, I can only help one person at a time. But if I go out and teach, I can help multitudes."

When Dave told me that, we started traveling a lot. The "arm" said that it would help people to be in his physical presence. He was not thrilled to learn that! He would have been happy just being at home, secluded, and writing the books, but he was always willing to do whatever he could to aid the evolution of others.

And, so, almost every Friday morning, we would drive two hours to the airport in Phoenix, and then get a plane to lecture at a different place. It was a demanding schedule for a person of any age, and he didn't start until he was 72. The last twelve years of his life were devoted to traveling, speaking, writing, and sharing himself. I think he lectured in a hundred different places.

His lectures laid out the whole way. He said that this earthly realm is a perfect place to learn and to evolve. Earthly life gives us a range of options, all the way from the worst cruelty to the incredibly angelic. It's up to us what we choose to live. He was here to guide us, and to help us learn how to discern truth from falsehood.

When we traveled, I saw how brilliant he was to speak in different ways to different audiences. One day he'd be speaking to an audience of science-minded people, and another day he'd be giving a sermon in a Christian church. One day he'd be blessing a group of Buddhists from South Korea, and another day he'd be answering questions with a delegation of Hindus from India. He had a way of connecting to the soul of anyone.

I want to share with you a few of the experiences we had while we were traveling and teaching.

Great Britain and Europe

One of my favorite trips was our month in Great Britain and Europe in August of 2003. Dave wanted us to do research in those places for his book, *Truth vs. Falsehood*, and he was invited to lecture there. We calibrated over seven thousand things for that book, including art, cathedrals, music, history, politics, and so forth. I thought my arm would fall off!

Our first stop was Ireland. We wanted to see the beautiful *Book of Kells* (cal. 570) in the library at Trinity College. I could not believe my eyes. This "illuminated manuscript" of the Gospels was done by monks in the 800s. They used symbols to illumine the meaning of the scripture. Each page was made of vellum and looked like a lush, ornate painting, full of color and intricate drawings. It was magnificent. I can see why it's called the "treasure" of Ireland. I wish I had time to study all of its symbolism; it fascinated me.

The next place we visited was Scotland. We had a once-in-a-lifetime experience there. We heard the bagpipe concert of the Edinburgh Castle Military Tattoo, which is done once a year. If you went to any of Dave's lectures, you know that he loved bagpipe music. He said, "It is the energy of the heart. It is valor, bravery, and love of one's country." At certain lectures, we hired bagpipers to come and play, just so the audience could experience that energy of the heart. When he was younger, David learned to play the bagpipes, but when he cut his thumb off with a saw, that ended his bagpiping career!

Here's what Dave wrote, in *Truth vs. Falsehood,* about our experience there in Scotland:

The Edinburgh Castle Military Tattoo (cal. 505) is an annual event that draws many thousands of spectators from all over the world. More than one thousand performers from the world's major countries represent their cultures' most skilled and highly trained military bands and precision drill teams. Their performances are breath-taking, and the huge crowd of spectators becomes silent with respect for the high degree of excellence displayed (e.g., the Swiss drum teams). Then to their surprise, the spectators begin to cry from the upsurge of a deeply stirring emotion (cal. 520) that is the energy of honor, valor, and love for one's human heritage and its representation as family, culture, and fellow man. The male bonding in war is at calibration level 510 (World War II). At the end of the Tattoo, one hundred bagpipes play "Queen of My Heart," which calibrates at 525 and leaves the audience in a state of awed silence at the surprising and unexpected upsurge of deep, profound emotion.

What he doesn't tell you is that the weather was wild, which added to the effect. We started off in a swelter of record heat, and then it poured rain and turned freezing cold. By the end of the evening, we were wrapped in sweaters and blankets. I had "chills" the whole time, and not only from the weather. The music gave me goosebumps.

At this concert, the first thing you see is the lone bagpiper in the distance, standing on the ledge of the castle, surrounded in smoky mist. He is playing that hauntingly beautiful bagpipe sound that sears into your soul. Then suddenly, hundreds of other bagpipers, drummers, and other players come out of the woodwork and swell the sound to great heights. You feel your soul soaring. I can hardly put it into words. Dave and I wept from the emotion of it.

When the music concert is over, you walk down the "Royal Mile" to Holyrood Castle, and you get to see the bagpipers right there, mingling and talking with everyone. It was a very special experience for Dave and me.

Dave loved music. His father was a talented musician, and Dave himself played several instruments—bagpipes, violin, piano. Dave and I calibrated all kinds of music. Music that calibrates at 500+ on the Map has a healing and uplifting effect. It wipes out negative thoughts and emotions. If anyone was depressed, Dave told them to watch the music video of *Riverdance* (cal. 500) because it lifts you out of a negative place. He also liked dancing to the Bee Gees (cal. 510)! If you are feeling down, remember that music and laughter are good medicine.

In London, we visited Westminster Abbey (cal. 790) where Dave had given a talk many years prior. We got there after they had closed at 3 p.m., but Dave found a way to enter into the back area so that he could show me where he had given his talk. The guard stopped us and said, "You can't be in here." I told him, "Oh, I'm sorry, my husband was just showing me where he gave a lecture. May we...?" He was kind and allowed us, which was wonderful because I wanted to say prayers there. You could feel the energy of prayer and devotion, and of all the great beings who had been there. But I'll have to say it was an eerie feeling walking on the graves of people like Winston Churchill!

We didn't have a lot of time in London because we had to get to Oxford for Dave's lecture. We stayed in a hotel at the University of Oxford, and so we got an exposure to college life. There was no bathroom in our room, so at 1 a.m. we were traipsing down the hallway, like you do in a dorm. The next day, someone broke into our hotel room. Nothing was stolen, no cameras or jewelry or anything, but it really shook me up. The staff said it was probably someone looking for drugs hidden in our room. Then, the night before Dave's talk, there was a Shakespeare performance on the lawn outside and people were yelling in the alleyway till the wee hours. College dorm life! Through it all, Dave remained calm, and his calmness helped me to stay calm.

Dave gave a marvelous talk at Oxford. At the end of it, we were standing with some of the other speakers, and two East Indian people from the audience came up and prostrated to touch Dave's feet. As soon as they did that, everyone around us gasped! It was a big inhale of shock, like they had never seen anyone prostrate like that before. Maybe they were horrified to see this happen in an academic town like Oxford, England. I myself was surprised by it, but I understood it was their custom, and it was very moving to see their devotion. They recognized David as an enlightened being. In certain countries, it is their custom to prostrate and touch the feet of a spiritual teacher. Even though Dave never wore any robe or special "guru" clothing, they knew what he was, and they felt compelled to bow in that way. They had hoped for a healing. One of them had come through two hernia operations. The other one also had health problems. They asked Dave how they could heal their problems. Dave gave his usual wonderful advice—mental, spiritual, and physical methods—and they went away happy, feeling that their prayers were answered. They were very heartfelt.

That act of devotion was repeated many times in the years to come. People at our lectures would want to prostrate or express their sincerity to David. He never asked for anything from his students. He was one with all; what would he have needed from them?! But if they asked to touch his feet, he allowed it. I think he saw it as helpful to their evolution. It wasn't about him. It was about helping *them*.

We were in France for a week and traveled on the trains to visit the cathedrals. Dave was very affected by Chartres Cathedral (cal. 790). It has a strong devotional energy field from many centuries of faithful people coming to pray. It is ethereal. He went into a high state and needed help to walk. Sainte Chapelle in Paris (cal. 735) was the place that gave *me* a big impact. I had a profound feeling of *deja vu* as I walked down the aisle, as if I had been married in that chapel in another lifetime. It was a very strong feeling. Somewhere in us, I think we recognize the journey our soul has made.

We visited museums like the Louvre in Paris (cal. 500) and the Rijks in Amsterdam (cal. 535) that has paintings by Rembrandt. Dave wrote about this part of the trip in *Truth vs. Falsehood*:

> The 500s reflect devotion to beauty and reverence for the great artistic creations of mankind. (Rembrandt calibrates at an amazing 700.) For centuries, millions of admirers have waited in line with awe for even a glimpse of such fabled greatness. The calibration levels are beyond those of the Newtonian paradigm with its gray steel desks and predictability, rising to the subjectivity of love, devotion, reverence, and intuiting the source of perfection. A visit to the Louvre in Paris is treasured by almost everyone.

As you can see from the calibrations, my arm got a workout during this trip! We visited many places each day, and then as soon as we got back to the hotel room, he wanted to calibrate the long list of things that we had seen. He was dedicated to giving you a book of calibrations that was comprehensive. He knew it would make your discernment stronger. *Truth vs. Falsehood* gives you guidance on every aspect of human life. I look back on that now in amazement. How did he know all of that? Some of what he calibrated was far ahead of its time.

Dave would be shocked that people now use his name and his calibration method for a fee, or to advance their own careers. People contact our office about this every week. One of our sincere followers told me that she attended an event with a so-called teacher who was referring to David's work as a way to get people to enroll in his own program of kinesiology for thousands of dollars! Other students of the work have told me about a website that charges a subscription fee for calibrations! I tell them: "If someone is asking you for a fee or a subscription to calibrate something, then it's a scam." It's not possible to get accurate answers using the kinesiologic method unless the intention is pure.

David was pure. His intention was to be of service to God and to help mankind.

Stories from the Road

Even strangers picked up on Dave's purity and his energy. We'd be in airports or restaurants, and people would just come up to us and start talking. They were people with spiritual insight, even if they didn't know who he was as a spiritual teacher and author. It was very interesting how many times that happened in a public place. I don't know whether they felt the Presence or what drew them. Sometimes we had to "rescue" him from people who would be just talking and talking to him. They wanted to be close to him.

Sometimes people even "came on" to Dave. In his teachings, he told us that people might do that. They would feel the love coming from his aura and confuse spiritual love with physical attraction. One time we were in San Francisco, and we had gone to an opera. Afterwards, Dave walked outside onto the patio. I was standing back because it was really cold and the wind was blowing. A man walked up to Dave and asked him for a light and said, "Are you by yourself?" It was a proposition. Dave said, "No, my wife is over there," and he pointed to me in the dark. And the guy said, "Oh okay," and walked off. Dave said to me, chuckling, "I'm 70 years old and they're still hitting on me!" He had compassion for the guy and said, "He was lonesome, looking for love."

Another time, after we'd given a lecture, people came up to ask questions. A woman approached Dave, pushing out her chest, wiggling her hips, and in a dripping sensual voice, she asked, "Can you calibrate with *me*?" I was standing there, just waiting to see what Dave would do. He said, "Well, no, I usually do it only with Suzie," and so the woman said, "Oh, but can you do it with me too?" She was very forward, like sex on a stick! Dave said, "No, I'm not going to do any calibration with you." In that moment I remembered what he said in his teachings, that teachers face these temptations.

He outlined the temptations many times. Money, sex, and fame are the three big traps for spiritual people, especially spiritual teachers. All three of these are forms of power over others, and a way to feel special. They are seductive, and we have to watch out for these temptations. Dave said that each of us has a certain one, out of the three, that we are especially vulnerable with. He told us again and again that whatever loving energy we have, it is not personal but divine. It is a big mistake to think, "Oh wonderful me!" and then take the money, affection and esteem coming from others. The problem is that most people are not even conscious of their motive for money, sex, or power; it's in their unconscious and so they project it onto others and don't see it in themselves.

Another instance of someone coming up to Dave was in the airport, but in this case, it was to almost arrest him! Dave was cutting up, having fun in his playful way. He loved to dance and clown around, make funny faces, sort of like a mime does as a street performer. All of a sudden, an airport security guard walked up to him and said, "Are you okay?" He thought Dave was acting suspicious. Dave instantly snapped to and became serious. "Oh yes, I'm fine, officer." And boy, he got out of that close call! He walked over to me and said, "I'm never going to do that in airports! I can't mess around like that. They thought something was wrong with me, and probably wouldn't have let me get on the plane!" This was soon after the 9-11 terrorist attack in 2001, and security was on high alert for unusual behavior.

Dave was his own person. He was brilliant but simple and kind—and he could talk like a sailor. He had been a sailor in the Navy, so he could let it rip! I remember one time we were getting ready to do an event at Unity Church. Dave was lined up to give the sermon for the church service that day. I said, "Now David, look, we're going to a church, so whatever you do, don't cuss!" And, of course, he did! I had to let go of worrying about it.

The Unity Church launched us to start speaking around the country in Christian churches. We gave all-day lectures at Unity Churches, which are free-thinking. The word began to spread.

Dave wasn't interested in making a name for himself or selling his books. He was only interested in reaching people, for them to learn from the work, learn about themselves and increase their spiritual awareness.

The only time we ran into a hostile person at a lecture was in New York City. What a wonderful city! I was so happy to see Central Park and all the beautiful areas in the city. Our event was at this little theater, one of the nicest ones I've ever been in. Dave was talking on stage and, suddenly, a man stood up and yelled from the balcony, "Oh, that's a bunch of bunk." Dave was shocked because it interrupted the lecture. The guy was up there, throwing his hands all around, and hollering down to the stage: "That's a bunch of bunk, and I don't believe a word of it." Everybody was shocked that someone would do this. Security went up to get him and walked him out. As he was being escorted out, I said from the stage, "We love you," and that was it. Nothing else to say. I was thinking, *Even though you're saying these terrible things, we still love you.*

I realized that someone will always criticize. So what? The critics can voice what they want. That's where they're at. We go on, sharing what we've been given to share, and it doesn't matter what people do with it. If someone criticizes me, I don't really care. But I do get upset when critics disparage the work, because I know how important it is to so many people. The work is reaching across the oceans to people in other countries. I'm glad to be a part of that.

During this time, when we were on the road and meeting so many people, they were asking us, "I feel stuck. How do I get to the next level?" So, I told Dave, "Listen, all these people are studying the Map, and they want to know how to move to the next level. Can you write a book on that?" And, so, he wrote the book, *Transcending Levels of Consciousness.* He whipped that book out fast.

We set up a big table in the living room. Our whole house was basically an office by now. He would get up sometimes in the middle of the night. He kept a little tape recorder next to our bed, and he'd say a word into it that would trigger what he wanted to write when he got up, something that he was dreaming about or thinking about it in the night. And then he would go in and write it out when he had a chance. He lived and breathed the work all the time. I'd wake up in bed at three o'clock in the morning, and he wasn't there. He had gotten up to write in the pitch black. He had one little light that he kept on the desk, and I'd see him sitting there, writing.

He wrote quite a few books like that—getting up around three o'clock, going back to bed at six and sleeping till ten. He was up for two or three hours a night. He liked to write when it was quiet and peaceful. He was devoted to doing all he could to help people heal and evolve. Three o'clock in the morning seems to be a magical time, a mystical time. I still wake up at three o'clock. Sometimes it's a call of nature! And sometimes it's a download of guidance.

Close Call

The "other side" is closer than we realize. The exact moment of death is set when we are born. That's what our research showed. In other words, our physical life ends when it's our time to leave the planet, and this moment is already set at birth. The means of death is not set, however. As Dave liked to joke, "You have freedom. You can stagger there or run there. Do it with an oxygen tank, or on a motorcycle. It's all up to you." One of his hobbies was to collect anecdotes about singular deaths. "When it's your time to go, you go!" He mentioned the case of the flight attendant who died while the plane was 36,000 feet up in the sky. The door suddenly opened, and she was sucked out, the only one out of 350 passengers. It's like God said, "Okay it's your time to go—right now!"

Dave and I had a moment when we thought it might be our time to go. It was a close call. We were on a direct flight from Phoenix to New York for a lecture event with the Learning Annex. Hundreds of people had signed up for the event. As we were flying over New Mexico, I looked out the window and saw the flames of the forest fires. It looked like the flames were touching the bottom of the plane! Our plane wasn't climbing in altitude. I thought,

There's something really wrong. Then the pilot came on and said in a serious voice: "We are experiencing plane difficulties. We'll have to make an emergency landing in Albuquerque." You could tell he was nervous under the calm exterior.

The plane cabin went into a dead silence. There was no panic or screaming. Dave and I just looked at each other and said, "The plane could go down any minute. Well, if it's our time, it's our time." It was surreal. I thought I'd panic, but I didn't. In the movies, when you see a plane is about to crash, everyone is screaming, but in actuality, there is a calmness that comes over you. When it's your time, it's your time, and there's nothing you can do about it.

The pilot came on again and told us to get into a "crash position." When we heard that, Dave and I just looked at each other like, "No problem. It's okay. We'll go together." The flight attendants came through and told everyone to put our pillow in our lap and lay our head on our pillow. "We'll let you know when it's safe to come up from that position."

Maybe because I was with Dave, I felt no panic. It was a total calmness. It was like a peaceful knowing that everything was going to be okay, no matter what happened. It was just that realization, looking into each other's eyes. At the time we didn't even say a word. We just held hands, looked at each other, and knew it was okay. We felt secure believing in God and knowing that everything was going to be okay, whether we lived or whether we died. It's a blessing to know that peace and security in your soul, to feel spiritually prepared for death.

Dave and I discussed this experience on our "Permanent Peace" video dialogue years later. He said it was a great example of how you can be in a state of peace "right in the middle of extreme danger." We were facing likelihood of sudden death, yet we were at peace with it. He said that's how he felt in World War II, on his minesweeper ship when the ship would bump up against an explosive mine or go through several days of a typhoon and the ship was tossed up to a 90-degree angle! In our dialogue, Dave said:

The fastest road to peace is total acceptance of the reality of however you're experiencing reality at that moment ... to accept the reality of your level of consciousness at all times, no matter what it might be.... I can be at peace with upsetness, because I accept that upsetness is appropriate at this moment. Like when we were afraid about the plane crash, we all accepted the fear, and nobody felt upset that they were fearful. We just accepted that. Yeah, sure, everybody's afraid they're about to crash. Because we were. Yet, there was a profound peace in the plane, even though people are about to die.... In fact, we were so much with the reality of the moment, that it was almost disappointing when we landed safely back—to the usual anxieties! We had the peace of the possibility of sudden death, and now we have the anxieties of normal life!

Dave put it in that funny way. It was true—we were in a state of peace when we knew we were about to die, and then when it passed, we were back to being concerned with the upcoming event, dealing with travel delays, etc.!

As we approached Albuquerque, we saw fire engines lined up on both sides of the runway. They had the hoses out, ready to spray slurry all over the landing field. Our plane's landing gear wasn't working, and they thought the brake system might catch fire. The landing went without a hitch, however, and nothing happened. They didn't even have to spray.

When you go through an experience like that, looking death in the eye, it wakes you up, and you ask yourself if you're doing what you're supposed to be doing with your life. There's a reason for you to be here on Earth; are you fulfilling your purpose? Those are the questions that come up after a close call like that.

When the time comes for you to die, you look back over your life and ask yourself, "How much time did I devote to spirituality?" I don't want to be one of those people who looks back over my life and wonders, "Did I devote enough to spirituality and to the betterment of mankind?" I want to look back and say, "Yes, I have."

That's a question everybody has to ask themselves: "Have I done everything I can in this life to better myself and to help mankind?"

You never know when you're going to go, so it's important for people to ask themselves that right now. "If I were to leave right now, could I say that I have done all I can to benefit mankind and the spiritual advancement of people around me?" That's what Dave and I worked hard to do. We have tried to benefit the spiritual advancement of everyone around us.

Questions and Answers

Q: What was your most awkward moment when you were traveling with Doc?

A: Probably in Korea. I wasn't used to certain foods. When you travel to another country and you have such wonderful hosts, sometimes you have to adjust yourself to new kinds of food. Dave and I were asked to attend a formal dinner with some important people—dignitaries similar to our members of Congress here in the States. Everyone was seated around the table, and they were eating different kinds of raw fish. I had never eaten raw fish, so I ordered soup. I thought that soup would be something familiar to me. Well, guess what? I was drinking this soup—you drink it like you're holding a cup—and all of a sudden, something slimy slid down my throat! I probably turned three shades of green and then three shades of grey, and I looked at Dave and said in a whisper, "Oh my gosh, something slimy went down my throat." And he whispered back, "Oh, that's entrails from those little spiny things that walk along the floor of the ocean—sea urchins." What a shock! I tried to hold myself together. I didn't want to get sick and throw up, because there was an important dignitary sitting across the table from me. Now, as I'm telling you this, I can laugh about it, but at the time, it sort of unhinged me. I'd never eaten entrails before, and of course that is a delicacy there and it was part of their being such gracious hosts.

Q: Was Doc here only for us, to help us evolve? In other words, he didn't need to come back for himself, did he?

A: He told me one time that he hadn't wanted to come back for this lifetime. And I was told by someone that I hadn't wanted to come back for this lifetime either. So, it was kind of funny, that neither one of us had really wanted to come back, maybe because we knew what was in store. So, you know, it's a learning process.

I don't think I can learn everything in one lifetime to do the good that I want to do, so I'll probably come back. After seeing what happened with Dave when he passed, it will be seamless. I think that's the way we'll go, just drift off, and into our next life, or our next body or whatever you believe in. If you only believe in one lifetime, we're only here for the one body, then you better make it count!

Q: Other spiritual teachers die and then their followers set up an institution to carry on that teaching in a formalized way. But here, it doesn't seem like that has happened. Why is that?

A: Doc said the teaching should go by "word of mouth." The teaching is transmitted through the energy, going by word of mouth. Like I mentioned before, Wayne Dyer called Dave and said, "We want to make you famous. We're gonna do this book and blah blah blah..." And Dave goes, "Oh ... I don't know about that." I heard it while he was on the phone. I was standing right there. Dave said, "I think it should go by word of mouth." And Wayne Dyer himself said, in a joking manner, "Dang it, I hate people like that—so pure!" Because Dave was simple, and he was humble. He wasn't into creating an institution. It's what Dave believed in, "attraction, not promotion" and that the work would go to the people who need it. We have his foundation that preserves the purity of his work and makes sure it is available to people when they are ready for it.

Q: Can you tell us something about muscle testing? You have obviously done zillions of the calibrations!

A: I'll tell you, the hardest book that we ever put out was *Truth versus Falsehood,* which has thousands of calibrations in it. I thought my arm was going to fall off! He'd say, "I need the arm." And we would test something. We'd do a hundred calibrations in a row, and I'd say, "I can't do it anymore. I've got to rest." And here he'd come again, "I'm working on this, and I really need your arm." I might be in the kitchen trying to cook dinner, and here he'd come. As time went on, I got stronger. I think my right arm has a larger bicep, so yes, I can deliver a good hook!

The main thing with muscle-testing is that your intention has to be pure, not attached. You won't get accurate answers if you have a personal interest in what you're testing. Dave and I were a good team because we just wanted the truth.

Truth versus Falsehood was a very difficult book to write. He was trying to tell people how to deal with the lower levels when it's necessary to relate with them. For example, one thing he always said, "Never give an excuse. Just say 'No' if it's something you can't do." Usually people say "No" and then they give a reason. You don't have to explain. Let your yes be yes, and your no be no.

Q: Do you feel like you are sometimes relying on your intuition, actually, instead of needing to calibrate things?

A: I have a very good intuition. I will have to say that. But when I used the arm with Dave, I was blank. I had no emotion or viewpoint about the question. I just heard the question. I had no say-so in how the outcome went, and I didn't want to influence anything. I heard the question, and that was it. Otherwise, you're not going to get the correct answer.

Now, with Dave gone, I have to do it like this (*O-ring test with her fingers*). Recently, for example, we were supposed to send some books to people in the Middle East, and they wanted *Truth versus Falsehood,* which I wasn't sure about sending so I had to calibrate it. And I got a "No" two days in a row. So I said, "No, we can't send that book to the Middle East. We might be able to at a different time, but right now, we can't do it." They were upset, but you have to stand your ground. And a lot of people, if they get a "No" on something, they don't like the answer, and so they say, "Let's do it again and see if we get a different answer"!

It's wonderful that all of you have read the books and are working on yourself. I'm just so proud of all of you. It fills my heart with gratitude.

Q: There is a group that says it is aligned with Dr. Hawkins' teaching, and they tell us to keep a secret, sign a pledge ... is that right?
A: No, no, no, no, no. Dave always said, "There's no secret." What are they hiding? Why are they binding you? When you get that feeling and it feels not right, then you leave. There are a lot of imitators out there and they're using his name to get you to follow them.

Q: But this is what's going on. If you get into this group, you make an agreement that you're not going to share that you're in this group or open up about it. It felt like a red flag to me.
A: It sounds controlling. David told us to be "anonymous," not secretive. He liked the 12-step model for our groups, which is to be *anonymous*, but not secretive. It's just like the book, *The Secret*. Dave flipped out when he saw that book. It's all about getting what *you* want—"manifesting" something for *yourself*, using "spiritual" techniques to get your ego's desires. And then they made a movie based on it. A "secret" group appeals to specialness. Dave taught us that whatever we're seeking is already inside of us. Perhaps the biggest secret is that there is no secret! The Truth is available to all who seek it.

9

LIFE IN THE PUBLIC EYE

Dave knew he didn't have a lot of time left, so he kept busy to complete the body of work that he wanted to leave for us. I don't remember a single day that he wasn't doing something related to the work. When he wasn't traveling or giving a lecture, he was at home writing another book, doing live radio interviews, or recording several audio programs. He was making notes about an upcoming lecture and contemplating student questions. He prayed for his students, and he prayed to be of service. And, of course, every day, he was giving my arm a strenuous workout! I'd be standing in the kitchen peeling potatoes or on the phone, and here he'd come, "Honey, I need your arm for something."

He was very inspired by people's testimonies that the teachings helped them. That's why we went out into the public to share the work in the first place—because it helped people so much.

But, as they say, "No good deed goes unpunished!" And, so, we had to deal with the problems that go along with sharing yourself in public. When you become any kind of known author or speaker, then people come out of the woodwork to ride your coattails, criticize you, or get something from you. Especially if you are a spiritual author, people think that you owe them your presence and your insight.

"No Trespassing"

People showed up at our house, insisting they had to see Dave. Some people thought he a miracle worker: "I need him to heal me."

Some people wanted him to transmit enlightenment to them: "I have to see Dr. Hawkins or else I'll never reach enlightenment." Still other people wanted him to know about *their* work: "I have to show my book to Dr. Hawkins." People had their various demands.

We ended up having to put up a security gate just to safeguard our privacy. People were walking up to our house and demanding to see Dave. We live out of town in the country, so it was surprising how they even found us. That was our first inkling that the work was getting out into the world. People were hearing about it and reading Dave's books. They thought they could come to the house whenever they wanted to.

One time, we had to leave the gate open for a shipment delivery, and in walked four people, right past the "No Trespassing" signs. They came up to our house and said, "We're from Germany and we want to see Dr. Hawkins!" Where is the respect and courtesy for the teacher? Dave was so generous to be out in public, in all of these places, and at his age it was not easy. And then he had to deal with people invading his privacy? It was not pleasant. Like the story I mentioned earlier, Dave would usually shut the door in their face!

Some of the people were unstable. One day, we were busy getting ready to do an event for the Koreans at the Creative Life Center, and out of the blue appeared a man standing outside of the gate. He kept ringing the bell to get in. He pleaded into the intercom, begging to see Dave. He was very insistent that Dave had to come out there and talk to him. We told him to leave the premises, and we found out later that he had mental health problems. Thankfully, Dave was a psychiatrist, and he understood the various conditions that make a person behave erratically. We never judged the people. We had compassion. But we also knew we couldn't ignore any kind of harassment or threat.

Over the years, there were many cases of people demanding or threatening us, and it was often due to mental illness. You realize that people cannot help their condition, but you also realize that you have to protect yourself because you never know what the condition might cause them to do. To illustrate this, Dave told me a story about when he was a psychiatrist in New York, and he had a patient who was just certain that Dave was having an affair with his wife. The man was delusional about it, and he was threatening Dave. The police caught him within a block of Dave's house, intent on harming him.

As a psychiatrist for many decades, Dave had been through harrowing moments like that, so he knew what to expect. He'd seen patients suddenly become violent. When he was working at the girls' correctional facility, one of the residents suddenly socked him in the face. He knew about such things, but, for me, it was new territory and I found it unsettling. One disturbing experience happened right after Dave passed away. Someone sent us an onslaught of emails claiming to have "killed the avatar." Who wants to get that in your email inbox, just after your husband has passed?

Dave warned me to be on the lookout for people who were unstable. Often they are not aware of their condition, he said, and they don't see a need for medication. He told me to watch out for clues and use discernment. We always tried to be helpful to people, but we also had to protect the people coming to our events. Because of his medical training, Dave was a pragmatist. He didn't want to take any risks. We used the arm to calibrate the various cases.

One time, a man from Europe kept sending us threatening letters. He'd written a book and he insisted that he had to read his book, in person, to David. He refused to mail it to us. He said he had to meet with David and read the book to him. We tested the arm on it, and it said not to meet with him. We told him, "No." But he came anyway, all the way from Europe. He sat outside of our gate, buzzing the ringer to get in. He came back three days in a row, and just sat out there in our driveway. Basically, we were being stalked and harassed, so we had to get a restraining order. This experience gave me compassion for people who are movie stars or famous in some way. They can't even leave their home to go to the grocery store, and they have to be careful where they go to eat dinner with their family.

Nose, Nuts, and Knees

Finally, we had to hire security for our events. We were getting hate mail from threatening people. At first, we didn't think too much about it, but then we heard that a well-regarded scientific speaker had been stabbed on stage by someone who had flown from the other end of the globe just to attack him. That's when Dave said, "Okay we'll have to get security." Why anybody would want to hurt a scientist or a spiritual teacher, I have no idea, but they're out there. Someone even shot John Lennon. So, Dave decided we had to be realistic and take certain measures to protect ourselves. He was aware, as a psychiatrist, that all it takes is one unstable person to do one rash thing, and then you wish you had gotten the security guard.

We had a wonderful couple in our group who were security experts. They trained police personnel for a living. The two of them were the security at many of our events. He would be on stage with us, and she would be at the back of the audience doing surveillance. We felt so fortunate to have them on our side, there to protect us and teach us how to protect ourselves in a crisis. They trained me in how to handle various scenarios, like if a violent person charged the stage. They told me, "Always hit at the three ends—nose, nuts, and knees!" And they taught me to be cautious in going out to our car, or coming home, always watching out for signs of strange behavior.

Believe me, this isn't what I imagined I'd ever have to learn—kneeing an attacker in the nuts! So, I want to say that the spiritual realm isn't all lovey-dovey, hearts and flowers! There is a downside to being in the public and giving spiritual lectures. One time a woman asked me, "Why do you look pensive when you're up there on stage with Doc?" Well, if you're reading this, now you know!

Dave was incredibly giving as a person. He wanted to help every being in any way that he could, but he also knew he couldn't do that at the expense of his own wellbeing. I learned from Dave that you have to safeguard yourself and your time. Your personal life isn't yours unless you demand it. As a teacher and author, he needed time for himself. We all need time for our own work and for our body and soul.

It takes away from all of us when our teachers have to devote this much time and money to protect themselves and their work. And oftentimes, it's protection from people who claim to be their students! That is why Dave was reluctant to go public with sharing his work, because he knew what people's egos would do with it.

I was naive at the beginning. I was very happy that so many people were coming to the lectures and getting something positive from it. Then I had a rude awakening. Some people were lying to our face, just to get in for free—not once but many times! It really shocked me what so-called spiritual people did with the work. They would steal, demand, and use it for their own gain. I had to learn that you can't trust people just because they're coming to a spiritual event. To be honest, it was crushing at first. I felt disappointed in mankind. It has been one of the hardest lessons for me not to lose my faith in mankind when I've seen what "spiritual" people do without a second thought.

Sometimes it's a minor thing, yet the attitude behind it is troubling. Dave taught me that some people are "takers," and some people are "givers." For example, when Dave was alive, we occasionally allowed a small group of devotees from different countries to come visit with Dave at the ranch. They made that request, and he wanted to honor it because they were making a big effort to come. It was exhausting for him, but he did it. We have some shells and rocks at the front of our house. One of the visitors said, "Can we have some shells?" I was thinking to myself, *Okay, they'll each take a shell,* so I said yes. They each took handfuls of them! I was shocked they took that many shells from our yard. I realized it was my fault, because I didn't say, "Just take one." But, really, I could not have imagined they would grab so many!

Dave and I had to learn the surprising lesson that even spiritual people will be "takers." There we were, opening our hearts to people, and their attitude was to take anything they could. The ego is always greedy for something, even in the spiritual realm. They were not aware of what they were doing, and so that meant that we had to protect ourselves.

Another example was when people would come up on stage as soon as Dave was done with the lecture and grab what they could. We had just given everything of ourselves to them all day, and they were coming to take something. We had to have a friend stand guard there, just to stop people from taking Dave's chair cushion or the flowers from the bouquet someone had given us for the event. They even wanted his Diet Pepsi can or the Kleenex box that he had touched. Were they going to sell it on the internet or what? Embalm it as a relic? They were trying to "get" something for themselves. I think there's a Buddhist teaching that says, "Don't take anything unless it's offered to you." It's a good one to remember.

Also, Dave was the example of someone who was always courteous and considerate of others. He never grabbed anything for himself. He told us, "Let others go in front of you." Instead of trying to get ahead—even spiritually!—what about offering to help others? Instead of being first in line so you can save seats for your friends in the front, what about trusting that God will place you where you need to be? Instead of wanting more, what about offering to give something?

I understand the longing. People felt they just couldn't get enough of him. It's because they felt loved in his presence. So, they wanted anything they could get that would remind them of this deep feeling of love—shells from his driveway, Kleenex, or Pepsi can! At some point, though, we have to let go of the outer objects and find that infinite love within our own Self.

So many people wanted to hug Dave that he finally had to say, "No more hugs." He was wearing a vest to keep his vertebrae from collapsing. One time a man hugged Dave and it broke his ribs. Dave didn't say anything about it to the man, because he didn't want him to feel bad, but it took him a while to recover from that hug!

Being in the public eye was wonderful. We loved the people, and we felt the joy of fulfilling the responsibility we felt to share the work. At the same time, we had to protect ourselves. To this day, sage and incense never cease burning at our house.

Questions and Answers

Q: Did you ever feel like you had to hide what he was from people?
A: I wouldn't say hide. I would say protect.

Q: Were there people who questioned if Doc was a real teacher?
A: There were skeptics. They are still around! There are always people who say, "Oh that's just a bunch of bunk." Well, it's easy to say that if you've never experienced the person and the teachings. Or maybe it's just not your thing. Or it's also the case that people project their own ego onto Dave. You have to be open in your heart to a certain extent in order to understand that he wasn't doing it for himself. Not at all. I've never seen David be selfish, ever, on anything. People can't fathom that. They assume he is like they are, run by ego, and that he's doing all of this to get something.

Even when Dave was so tired, and I knew he was about ready to collapse, he'd give *more*. We are all blessed for having him show that to us. I got to see it, but it wasn't just me. He shared himself with everybody. There was no switch that was on and off. There was nothing fake about how he was in the public eye with all of you; he was like that all the time. I'd come into the house after a long day and say, "I'm done—I don't want to do this anymore!" But then he'd say two words to me, and I'd say, "Okay, okay let's do it." He'd say, "It's gonna be fine. Don't worry about it." And he was always willing to give until he collapsed. Giving himself all the time, extending himself to answer all those different questions—it was very emotionally draining. And he gave it to all of us.

His teachings are true, and that's what he was. He wanted all of us to become better people. He wanted to give us every chance and every tool to learn what we needed to learn so that we could overcome our suffering. He taught us how to evolve. He coined the term "Homo spiritus." And he taught us how to become that.

That's why he chose "teacher," instead of avatar or guru or any of the modern titles that people use. He said, "I'm not any of those. I'm just a teacher. That's it." So he chose a profession that everybody hates!

You know, I feel sorry for our teachers in the education systems. They don't get the pay they deserve and they're teaching overbooked classes and they're trying to communicate with students who are struggling. It's very hard to be a teacher of young people.

For Dave, he was teaching about his experiences in consciousness and of the higher realms that are not experienced by many people.

Q: When *Truth vs. Falsehood* came out, did you have any repercussion from that?
A: No, we didn't get much blowback on that, but somehow we got on the mailing list of a radical political group that sent us a box of their books. They were very strange books. We called the FBI and told them about the books, and we ended up sending them off to the FBI. And we were getting emails from some guy who was just ranting about the government. We didn't answer it. He said, "I'm taking you off my email list," and I thought, *Good Riddance*! All of these were bizarre groups.

Q: I've heard there are websites that lambast Doc's work. How do you keep yourself sane when you see what people say about Doc or how they twist his teaching?
A: I don't! *Laughter...* It's really hard. Because when you reach a certain level, it pulls up the opposite. I've learned that lesson and it's a hard one. Dave warned me it would happen. It's one thing if someone disagrees with you. Okay, that's fine. But some of the critics are mean and nasty. They'll take anything you say and twist

it around. You have to develop a thick skin. And some of these people never even met Dave or saw him or read his books. They don't even know what they're talking about. They're just criticizing to criticize. It would be hard to be in his presence without realizing what he was, in actuality. I also know a few of the critics who are just plain jealous of David and his degrees and his accomplishments. They like to use his name, even if it's to criticize, because then it brings people to their website. It's an internet manipulation. If you criticize someone famous, then you get attention and money that you wouldn't otherwise get! It's very strange.

Q: What did you learn from Doc about unconditional love?
A: It was hard for me because I saw the downside of it when Doc was in that state. You know how in his lectures, he'd say there's a downside to each level. Unconditional love leaves you vulnerable because you see only the good in everybody. Dave trusted everybody, and there were people who took advantage of him. He would say, in his unconditional love, "They would never do anything to hurt me," but then we'd end up in a mess because they betrayed him. I never said the words, "I told you so," but I felt like it a couple of times! That was the hardest thing I had to do—see someone hurt him because I had not said, "I've got a bad feeling about this." After he became well-known, there were people that came into our lives who didn't have our best interests at heart, so I learned I had to speak up more. Dave relied on my "woman's intuition"—that's what he called it.

I don't personally think I could live in that state of unconditional love all the time and also do the work I have to do here. At the level of Unconditional Love (540), like Dave said, you can't function in a normal life. You can experience that level at different times in your life, and you can be there for a while, but I don't think you can *live* there and survive in this world unless you are in a protected environment like an ashram or you have people helping you. Dave had me to buffer him and take care of the world for him. I don't have a buffer. Maybe next lifetime!

The hardest thing for me to see is someone's ego standing in the way. I've been seeing it more lately, and I don't know what brings it out so clearly. I guess I've been having to deal with the public so much that it confronts me more. I get more upset by it than I should. I notice that people think they are very spiritual, and yet to their own children, they're not kind, they're mean. And I see people that think they are kind, but they're only kind when someone is looking. Dave always said to me, "Don't let it bother you. They'll show their true colors eventually." It's just the spiritual warrior that comes up in me sometimes when I see something that's so off-base. I want to say something, but I don't, because I know it's better to let it go.

I think it's also that, as women, our instinct is to protect what we love. It's an instinct that we are born with, to protect our loved ones. It's biological. So, we have to learn to stand back sometimes, like when your baby is learning to walk. You have to stand back and let them fall a few times, and then they'll learn. It hurts to see them fall, but that's how we learn. We have to let go wanting to save other people. That's because our rescuing them actually prevents them from learning what they need to learn.

Dave was a great example of that. He never gave advice to the people around him. One of our close friends told me, "Every once in a while, I'd ask his advice on something, and he was just silent. He would never tell me what to do." He let people come and go and do their own thing. If you try to prevent people from living their life, then you're a cult. People have their free will. For example, we had a young man who was with us for a few years; he helped us around the ranch, drove us, helped us at events, and became almost like a son. But he was young, and he had to go and live his life. We didn't give him advice or ask him to stay. He got what he needed here. His life turned around because of Dave's teachings. And then it was time for him to go and fulfill his destiny elsewhere. So, you see, when you love people, you let them go, you let them live their own life. You want them to grow. You don't cling or tell them what to do. I'd say that's the essence of the teaching on unconditional love that I learned from Dave.

Q: What was it like for you when people took advantage of Doc, or criticized him?

A: He was a very trusting soul. When I first came here to be with him, I could see that people were using him, which was very sad, but it wasn't my place until we were married to say anything to him about it.

Whenever you reach a high state, you always have the lower state that will come up to counter it. It's human nature. People from a lower energy field will come up and say that they know it's different than what you're presenting. You have someone who is high in their wisdom, and someone else comes along and says, "No, that's not right." They don't have any basis to it, but they'll pick out the things they want to argue to make their story plausible. They will always find something that you're saying or doing that's "wrong" according to what they've selected to pick on. They like to pigeon-hole you.

I feel sorry for the Royals, for example. These poor young kids on the front page every time you turn around, and people are always judging them and the mothers: "She's a good mother, she's a bad mother, she's this, she's that." I feel sorry for them, because they're living under scrutiny and judgment for the rest of their lives.

Even if you do good work, people are always going to criticize you. Even if you do your very best at whatever it is, there's always going to be a critic. I mean, look at Mother Teresa. Some guy wrote a negative book on her too, and she was a saint.

Seeing these things happen to Dave and to the work—it motivates me to work even harder. I have found that anger can be a stimulant, so in the end, it makes me work harder for what I love.

PART IV:
LIVING THE WORK

LETTING GO

Dave passed away ten years ago. It has taken me this long to share something about it. If you've lost a spouse or loved one, then you know how hard it is to put certain experiences into words. I will try my best to do that for you, because many of you have asked me about his last year.

The main thing I want to say is that Dave died just like he had lived—doing his best to help others. He wanted to make sure that, before he left this planet, he had personally answered any question that would come up, so that there would not be any confusion as to his intention or teachings.

We worked for over twelve years to complete his body of work. It's a very significant body of work, and we did it out of love for God and mankind. I was the arm that he used to test everything, thousands of times! I can still feel his two fingers gently pressing down on my arm. We have given our lives to make his teachings available to all of you.

Completing His Work

During Dave's last year, he worked to complete his body of teachings, through lectures, satsangs, dialogues, books, and interviews. His largest lecture was on "Love," in September 2011. We had to drive an hour away to Prescott to find a big enough venue for the 1700 people who came from around the world.

The weeks before his Love lecture, his body was giving out. He had picked up a virus from someone at the prior month's satsang, and then the doctor diagnosed him with dehydration. I wasn't sure he'd even survive to do the lecture. His health revived when I made him drink water and electrolytes in between his espresso and Pepsi! Still, we had to use a wheelchair to bring him on and off the stage at the Love lecture. He was 84.

Leading up to the Love lecture, Dave sang "Sing Song Kitty" around the house. It is a nonsensical little ditty that Dave's father taught him when he was a boy. He wanted everyone to know it. He said it was an example of how, out of our love for someone, we are willing to learn something by heart and never forget it. Dave remembered that ditty for 80 years, out of love for his father. "Sing Song Kitty" was the first thing he shared on stage at the Love lecture. He sang it for us in his vibrant playful spirit, giving a great example of how something learned out of love never leaves you. It was amazing. Everyone cheered. He intended it as a deep lesson. "He who has ears to hear, let him hear."

Due to failing eyesight, he wasn't able to read his lecture slides on the screen, so we asked our friend to read for us. He and I sat at the table together and dialoged on the points that were being read. I asked him questions, and he answered. We'd never done a lecture this way, but it worked fine. We were in sync with each other, engulfed by the love of everyone there. There were many moments during the lecture when we both wept. We were touched by what we were sharing, and by the momentousness of the gathering, with so many wonderful people and knowing it would be his final lecture.

One story he told was about a male duck that was shot by a hunter. The duck fell to the ground with broken wings, and then its mate swept down and opened her wings to shelter it. When the hunter saw this act of love, he gave up killing animals for sport. The love that the ducks had for each other was obvious. How can you kill a being that is loving and loves its life? Dave said it was the energy of the heart that convicted the hunter to give up killing ducks. That picture of the two ducks led thousands of other hunters to give up killing animals for sport. Every time Dave and I talked about that story, we wept. He also talked about our marriage as "mutual ducking." We take turns being either the duck that shelters the other, or the duck that needs to be sheltered.

There were a lot of tears shed at that lecture. During the final segment of the event, people from various countries shared their testimony. Thailand, Australia, England, South Africa, India, South Korea, and many more places were represented. We made time for this because we knew Dave couldn't speak for the entire six hours, and because people had requested a chance to express their gratitude. At the end, we had the bagpiper come on stage, and that was the finale. The bagpipe expresses the nobility of the heart that Dave lived and loved so much. I don't think there was a dry eye in the place.

It was the completion of his public life. He was too tired to speak any more. He was sitting in his wheelchair, exhausted. I stood with him there at the end and told everyone to share what they had become. People were crowded around the bottom of the stage. Dave had given them all they needed, and now it was time for them to *become* the teaching, and to pass that beingness on to others.

He lived for another year and accomplished more in that one year than many people do their entire lifetime! Still, he was definitely going through the effect of aging. He told me many times, "I've never been this old before!" Other lifetimes, he had died at a younger age. Old age was a new experience for him.

He'd always been an industrious man. When he was in medical school, he worked three jobs at once. In his last year of life, it was hard on him to not be able to see well. He was accustomed to reading a book a day, which he did for most decades of his life, but in the last year, we had to read to him. He loved working in his carpentry shop. He had built the waterwheel, chicken house, and cabins on the ranch. When his vision went downhill, he couldn't see the tools in his workshop. He said, "Just imagine you reach for the hammer and POW! it's a scorpion instead!"

He told our friend a few months before he passed:

> Losing vision in the right eye changed my life. I grew up with a Protestant ethic that said you always had to be busy, creating or making or doing something like writing a book, etc. What's left for me is to love. I try to love everything and everyone all the time. I don't have to have vision for that, or a piece a paper to write on. I spend most of my time in prayer, to be loving toward all things at all times.

I'm sure he would have been happy just to let the body go, but he was committed to fulfilling what the world needed from him. He did everything in his power to stay active. He went to physical therapy to strengthen his knee. He wanted to keep as strong and functional as possible. He told our friend, "Suzie has so much to do around here, and now she's got an old man to take care of. I love her too much to be lazy! The least I can do is get this knee back in shape, so I can save her from walking out to get the chicken eggs every day!" He did his knee exercises while he sat in his favorite chair to watch the news.

One of the projects he finished was the book, *Letting Go: The Pathway of Surrender*. He had written the first manuscript many years before I met him, but he'd given it to someone else and lost track of it. The typed pages ended up in a file box in a closet somewhere out in California. I remember Dave said to me at one point, "I wish I had that manuscript back." Out of the blue, someone contacted us and said, "I found this manuscript. Give me your address and I'll send it to you." So here it came back to him, twenty-plus years later! I thought it was a wonderful miracle. Everything has its perfect timing.

To be honest, Dave was getting tired, and he wasn't thrilled to work on a book he wrote so long ago. You have to understand that it was hard for him to squeeze himself back into the box of what he had been before. Plus, he felt like he'd already written enough books, but I told him, "Dave, I think this book will really help people. Let's do the arm on it." I knew he'd do it if it could help people. And sure enough, the arm tested that it was for the highest good to revise the manuscript and publish *Letting Go*. I'm glad he did that book. We hear from lots of people that it helps them heal and recover from many things. He felt fulfilled knowing that it helped people. "It won't cure stupidity, but aside from that, it'll get you over pretty much anything!"

He also finished interviews with his biographer. She came over to the house several times a week to meet with him. Sometimes I'd come home from the grocery store, and they'd be in his office working on a project. When I popped my head in, he'd wave his arms like it was an S.O.S., "Honey, help help! Save me from this lady! She's working me to the bone!"

When they worked on the *Letting Go* book, if I had the time, I'd sit and listen to them reading through the chapters and doing the revisions. Dave was brilliant in how he could make one small adjustment to the wording, and it changed the whole tenor of that passage. If you've read his books, you know how vast his vocabulary is. Many people say they have to look at a dictionary while they read *Power vs. Force*! That was another book project he finished. He wanted to publish his "Author's Official Revised Edition" of *Power vs. Force* before he left the planet. The first edition was published in 1995. A lot had happened with the work over those seventeen years, so he wanted to complete a final official revised edition.

Something else that was important to both of us was to video-record our dialogues on key topics for students of the work. Dave wasn't strong enough to keep up all the public lectures, but he enjoyed speaking if he and I sat and discussed a topic at home. We video-recorded eight "fireside" dialogues on topics like "Improving Your Relationships," "Permanent Inner Peace," and "How to Live Your Life Like a Prayer."

He would say, "Honey, I'm sorry I'm not as eloquent a speaker as I used to be, but the message is still there." His message is there for anyone who is ready for it, as timely as ever. Recently, I was listening to our dialogue on "Real Success," and it helped me to remember that sometimes success is just in our being there for others, or asking a question that helps them to grow. Here's an excerpt from our dialogue:

Q: Dave, is there anything else you want to say on "Real Success"?
A: I feel myself to be successful, that I have you in my life and that we've covered the setting here with a camera focused on us, and therefore more people other than just you and myself will be hearing this. I consider that successful, when your life is contributing to the life of others. So, to me, success is when your life is contributing to the life of others. If nothing else but stirring up the question in their own mind after they listen to us, and they say, "Well, what do I consider success to be?" It brings up the question in their life, and we all grow through the questions that we ask ourselves. So, the degree that we're helping other people to grow, I feel my love is in that success, and I thank you for making this a success.

Dave maintained his good humor even while going through old age. On the same day we did that video-taping of the "Real Success" program, a friend asked him, "Doc, what's your advice for success in old age?" He said, "1. Trust women's intuition. 2. Always choose peace. 3. And don't fart in public!" These are the kinds of things he said behind the scenes that made me laugh.

Another funny moment was when a friend asked him, "Hey, Doc, what did you have for breakfast this morning?" Dave responded in a flash: "Oh, an egg and bacon sandwich... I used to have 3 beers, 1 scotch, 1 whiskey and pretzels, and that would last me all day... but then someone told me it was unhealthy, so I gave up the pretzels!"

So, you see that we had a good time even while we worked hard! His humor kept us all light-hearted, and I think it was his way of dealing with old age. He complained a little bit, but mainly he tried to keep his humor about it.

Like most older people, Dave liked staying home. He didn't want to travel or go out much. If you've ever tried to move a person who is in their 80+ years out of the home they've lived in for decades, you know what I'm talking about. It just goes with the territory. Dave would say, "I can't see where I'm going when I'm out there in the world. At least if I'm home, I can *feel* my way around and eventually find the ketchup when I need it!"

And, so, when someone offered to install a new granite counter in the kitchen, and it meant taking Dave out of the house for a few days, he fussed: "Here I am, f****d by the fickle finger of fate once again!" But he told a friend, "If it makes Suzie happy, then let's do it." I had lived with a very old pink Formica countertop that whole time, so I was delighted to have a new countertop! I felt it was important to get the new one in while he was still living, so it had his energy. These are things you think about when you know your lovemate isn't going to be around much longer.

Dave had a way of reminding us of the essence of things. "Life is actually very simple. It's just difficult to remember that!" He was so profound yet so funny! He made this statement while he was lying in our living room in a hospitable bed. That is how he spent the last weeks of his life. He wanted to pass away at home.

Beginning of the End

Dave had a stroke on August 11, 2012, then he died in the evening on September 19, 2012. He was very adamant that he did not want to be left here by himself; he wanted to be the first one to go. We talked in detail about what would happen, especially when he knew that the body was failing. He told me how he wanted me to run the business and the foundation. We put everything into place in accord with his instruction.

Dave and I were at home when the stroke occurred. It was in the evening. He was standing at the fridge and then suddenly slumped over. I got him into a chair, and I saw he was leaning over to his left side. I knew he'd had a stroke. I called our two friends, and they came over. When you go through something like that, it helps to have your friends.

We called 911 and took him to the local ER. Dave was suddenly better when we got there, so the doctor was going to send him home. I kept saying, "No, there's something wrong." Sure enough, he had another stroke right there. The doctor then wanted Dave to have an MRI, so he called the hospitals in Cottonwood and Flagstaff, but they were full. That meant Dave had to be taken on air-evac to Phoenix. By this point, it was very late at night. One of our friends went with Dave on the helicopter, and the other friend drove me down to Phoenix after I took care of the animals at home. I remember weeping as we rode down to Phoenix, because I knew it was the beginning of the end. We got a hotel room, and we took turns staying with Dave at the hospital.

The hospital was calling in every doctor they could and trying to get the tests done, but Dave was just getting worse. They never gave him the shot for the stroke, even though I kept saying he'd had a stroke. His left side was semi-paralyzed. It was obviously a stroke, but they said he moved too much when they did the MRI, so they couldn't determine what had happened. I could see he wasn't going to get the help he needed there, and he just wanted to come home. Our friend got the hospital bed set up in our living room, and we hired an ambulance to bring Dave home from Phoenix. He was overjoyed to be home with our animals. The first thing he asked for was some espresso!

A few days after he was home, he went to the Cottonwood hospital to have a feeding tube put in, because he couldn't swallow well. He told me that's what he wanted me to do for him, so that's what we did. One of our friends stayed with him overnight in the hospital room and said that the nurses had to put in an emergency catheter during the night. These were unpleasant procedures, but they were the extra measures that Dave put himself through because he was committed to be in the body as long as he could be helpful to me and mankind. After he came home, he even worked with a physical therapist at home for three weeks, to see if he could re-energize his left leg and his left arm. He was hoping to walk again. There was a glimmer of possibility, but it just didn't happen.

Dave always did his best to be cheerful and loving to everyone. He was very happy to be home, even if he couldn't walk. The cats slept on his feet, and Kelsey knew where to sit by the right side of the hospital bed so he could give her treats with his right hand. One time there was thunder, and she jumped up on the bed with him!

That last month was really hard. If you've taken care of someone in your home, you know what it's like. And when it's your lovemate, there are so many different emotions. At one point, there were several nurses coming in and out of our home. I was grateful for the help, yet it wasn't easy to deal with the lack of privacy and different personalities. Whenever I could, I took care of Dave myself. Even though it was exhausting work, I was grateful for those times of quiet and privacy with him. He didn't like sleeping in the living room; he missed sleeping with me in our bed. I was aware I'd be losing him soon. I was numb from the shock of it all.

Thankfully, I got to have clear conversations with him about everything he was going through and what he wanted me to do for him, and for the work. He told me, "Just use your common sense, Suzie." We trusted each other. He had done what was needed to set up everything so that I would be taken care of. His responsibility was to me, so that I could carry on as the steward of his work.

Dave continued to do whatever he could that was helpful to the work and to others. He signed many cases of books for future students. We talked about emails that were coming in and decisions that had to be made. For example, right at this time, we had to deal with the fact that someone had written a negative book about Dave's life and claimed it was an authorized biography. The book lacked integrity. It violated Dave's express wishes. For Dave, it was a betrayal of trust. He said it was necessary for him to send an email to all his students, to tell them it was not an authorized biography. Dave was a man of his word, but he did not hesitate to change course if a situation called for it. A teacher can authorize something at one point in time, and then suddenly withdraw that authorization if needed. Over the years, there were several times that someone started out with a positive intention, working with us on something, but then it reversed, and we had to end it.

I think one of the reasons Dave stayed on the planet during the last month was so that he was still alive when that book came out and he could make clear his view of it. The very last email announcement that Dave sent out to all his students before he died was to let them know that this book was *not* an authorized biography. He told them he did "not endorse it." I'm sharing this with you here, because you may not have seen David's statement on it, and he wanted his students to know how he viewed it.

I asked him, "Why would someone do that?" He said, "He wanted to sell the book and get the money and the little bit of fame that went with saying those things about me." Negativity sells, just like on the news. People are curious, so they buy it. It's a sad society in that way, but it also serves the whole purpose of this world, in terms of karma. Dave told me to ignore the book, not take action on it, because things that lack integrity don't last. He said, "It's just a flash in the pan." And, so, we did not take legal action. It was not easy for him to go through that kind of betrayal at the end of his life. Dave regretted that someone whom he had trusted would disrespect him like that, but he also accepted it as God's will. He realized that his teachings on truth had brought up the opposite. He said this quite often, "When you get to a certain level, it brings up the opposite."

Dave turned everything over to karma. He said, "We'll surrender it to God and let karma handle it." And, of course, he made a joke about such folks, "Well, if they die and wake up in Walgreens, they'll know they messed up! It's not our problem. It's God's problem."

His Passing

We had many beautiful and peaceful moments. Our priest from the Episcopal church came over several times, to administer healing prayers and last rites. She said to Dave that he would probably "two-step" into Paradise; we laughed and laughed at that. The priest was going on a long trip to Europe, so our friend took a video of her administering the last rites, and we played it for Dave at the very end. Close friends came over in the evenings to say the evening prayers and read to him some of his favorite passages from the Bible like Psalm 91.

They brought Eucharist from the church to us in our home on Sunday mornings. Having that communion meant a lot to Dave. He would not eat anything on Sunday morning until after the communion.

At a certain point, I could tell that Dave wanted to leave. It was time to let go. I dismissed the nurses and everyone except our two close friends. The three of us nursed him for three days in shifts; one of us tended him while the other two were sleeping on the couch, trying to get a little rest.

On the morning of the day that he passed, we were exhausted and, to top it off, we suddenly had a septic problem. I can laugh about it now, but at the time, it was stressful. Dave would laugh at this, I am sure. It was his kind of humor. A friend told me that Dave had joked a few days prior, when she was cleaning him up: "Yeah, at the end, you poop out all your unworked karma!" Here's what happened the day he passed. The toilet backed up, so I had to call the plumber to come in and deal with it. Here's Dave on hospice in the living room, and the plumber is running through the house trying to get the shit cleared out!

While the plumber was there, I heard Dave say, "I smell angels." I asked him, "What are you smelling?" He said, "I smell roses. There are angels present. It's a sweet smell, very sweet, beautiful smell."

To the rest of us, it was smelling like a toilet overflow! He would have enjoyed the parody of it, the earthiness of it. It's funny now, but it was stressful at the time. I had reached my breaking point. I just didn't think I could go on any longer. I actually said to him, "David, you've got to go soon, because you're killing us!"

To see someone you love have to go through everything he went through, and then to have to tell him something like that to get him to pass on over, it sounds harsh, but he needed me to let him know it was okay to go.

Our friends said that he told them, "I'm staying here for Suzie." I don't know if he stayed for me, or if he stayed here because of the work. It was the same. He had completed his whole body of work. "I have nothing left to say." He'd written so many books and given so many lectures. He knew that I would continue with the work and fulfill my responsibility to safeguard it for the future.

The end drew near. He hadn't taken drugs or alcohol for over 40 years, not even analgesic during surgery. But he told me that morphine was the right thing to use at the very end, as a mercy for the body and those witnessing the death of their loved one, so that's what we did.

All the animals came into the room. They knew he was going. When he made the transition, it was seamless. He was here and then he wasn't. He went from being with us, to being with God. It was heartbreaking to see those beautiful blue eyes closed, but his peacefulness filled the room. It was a quiet peace that settled upon our home and stayed there for many days. His Spirit left the body, but it was still in the house. I felt it as a very strong presence in the days after he died.

We washed the body and clothed it in the special burial shroud that his students from South Korea had made for him. Dr. Moon had brought it to us two years prior. It was a golden robe with a hat and even little booties for the feet. They gave him gold because of who he was. Usually, it's white. The whole ashram sewed this robe for him. I had wanted to put him in his overalls because he loved them so much, but he said, "No I will do what the Koreans have prepared." It had to be folded and tied in a certain way. Dave's face was beatific and peaceful. When they took his body out of the house on the gurney, his Spirit stayed in our home.

Three days later, when we were at the mortuary for the cremation, Dr. Moon came to make sure that we had put the robe on correctly before they took his body into the crematorium. In his instructions to the mortuary, Dave asked not to be cremated for three days because of the fact that the body has to adjust to the transition. He told me that the Spirit would be at the ranch, and I can honestly say that I felt his presence at home for at least those three days, if not longer.

His passing showed me that our transition from this life to the next is seamless. You just leave this earth behind and go onto the next place. Another thing I learned from Dave's death is that hearing is the last thing to go. The person who is dying might not be able to speak, but they can hear you, so make sure that you tell your loved one who is leaving the body, that you love them before they go. I got to do that with Dave. The person, as they are passing, are both here and there for a while.

Dave was with Bill Wilson when Bill was getting ready to pass. He said that Bill would come in and out of awareness. Bill would say, "I've been to my Father's house, and there are many mansions." I think that tells us that, whatever we believe in, we will go to that particular "mansion." There isn't just a single place on the other side. Whatever we're blessed with as a religion or a belief, we go to that.

Dave's teaching is not a religion. It is a direct path to Truth. I think it's good to have some type of religious or spiritual "backup," something that provides you with your spiritual friends and community. His work can take you the whole way, but it's also helpful to have that spiritual or religious community to be with you as you go through the passages in life. Dave was born Episcopalian and he stayed a member of that church to the end. It meant a lot to him, and to me, that we had the blessings and prayers from the priests, and friends from the church who brought the Eucharist to our home. Dave was always crossing himself, "in the name of the Father, the Son, and the Holy Spirit." Even though he wasn't defined by religion, he appreciated the sacredness of these rituals. Whatever you are religiously or spiritually, it's helpful to have a community to support you.

In those last weeks, Dave would cross himself frequently and say: "What matters is that you feel cared for. As long as you feel loved and cared for, that's what matters. I'm surrounded by love. Thank you, Lord, for such a wonderful wife, great friends, a great doggie, a great birdie, and three adorable kitties."

After His Death

They say that your spiritual guides try to reach you at three o'clock in the morning. I think that must be true. I often feel Dave is here at three in the morning. Sometimes his presence is so strong, it wakes me up out of a sound sleep. It's like his words are coming to me.

It was very difficult for me after his death because I not only lost my husband and companion, but I also thought I'd lost my spiritual guide. You look to someone to help you understand the higher levels. After his death, I had no one to talk to in that same way. Now, all these years later, I can say I don't feel separated from him. I feel immersed in him.

We had built this spiritual body of work, with thousands of people following it, and David was the glue. When he passed, I was in no position to hold everything together. Spiritually, I was fine, but I was struggling in other ways. Physically, I was exhausted from the caretaking and from having to handle everything you have to do when your loved one dies. It was overwhelming. Emotionally, I was in shock. I was numb. It was like a depression. I think I just sat for three months and stared at the TV screen. I can't even tell you what I watched.

I know my own self. I am fine in crisis. It's afterwards that I fall apart. So, I got through the crisis of Dave's stroke, hospitalizations, hospice, all of that, pretty well. But after it was all over, I said, "Oh! How did I *do* that?" Dave always told me, "God's grace will handle it."

There was no way I could get right back into the world after his death. He was this beloved, exceptional person who loved his students and rattled their cage when they needed it, but now I felt alone with that heavy responsibility. A lot of people had moved to Sedona for the work, and after Dave passed away, they scattered to the winds. He told me that would happen. He also told me that his students would look for another teacher. "They like to have someone in the flesh." He told me to expect that some of his students would even try to step in to "presume" to be a teacher of his work. All of that has happened.

After Dave died, I had a lot of letting go to do. His book, *Letting Go*, arrived from the printer just a couple weeks after he passed away! Letting go sounds easy to do, but it's not. It's like a story that the priest told my friend who was getting a divorce. He said to her: "Did you ever hear about the guy who was a mountain climber? He had those pitons that they use to get inside of the cliff. Just as he got to the outcrop of the cliff he was climbing toward, he suddenly lost hold and he was just hanging from this rope with no way up and no way down. He was just hanging there! He yelled, 'Is there anybody up there?' And he heard: 'Yes. I'm God. Have faith and let go!' He was hanging from this rope. He looked up and he looked down, and then he yelled, 'Is there anybody else up there??!!'" That says it all, doesn't it? "Have faith and let go!"

Even during this difficult time, there were funny moments. Laughter helped me get through. One funny incident happened with Dave's box of ashes at the church's Columbarium. I have most of his ashes at home, but Dave wanted some of his ashes to be put into a simple wooden box and installed at the Columbarium of the local Episcopal Church. I got the measurements for his niche and paid the mortuary to have a carpenter build the box. My two friends and I picked up the box, put some of Dave's ashes in there, and headed to the Columbarium to have the special ceremony with the priest. It was the private ceremony that the church does when they install someone's ashes into the niche. The priest was saying the prayer as I'm sliding Dave's box into his niche, but it got stuck halfway. It didn't fit! I turned to the priest and said, "Oh that's just like Dave—he never fit in any box!" So, I had to take it back to be remade. We did the ceremony all over again, and Dave slid in just fine in the new box! After it was over, we released a bunch of balloons into the sky. It felt good to let go of those colorful balloons and watch them rise and rise and rise. One of them headed toward the ranch.

We were busy planning the funeral. Everyone said the funeral was beautiful, and it was. For me, however, it was more like an event, rather than a memorial service. It was one of the hardest things for me to do. I was still in shock from his death, and I had to put on a big event.

Dave loved the Episcopal cathedral in Phoenix. I knew he would be pleased by the beautiful setting and the fact that we had the Eucharist as part of the service. He was a veteran, so we asked a World War II veteran to attend in uniform and present the flag to me while "Taps" was being played on the bagpipe. That really got me. Dave's service to his country and his shipmates meant a lot to him. They almost lost their lives in a typhoon, and I think he was the last one from their crew to die.

My elderly mother and other family members wanted to attend. Mostly it was Dave's spiritual students who attended, and they came from all over the world. Everybody had to get hotel rooms, and they needed help from our office with logistics. It was a lot for me and my staff to organize. We wanted to make it work well for everyone.

The Koreans came dressed in their white dresses, which is what they display when they are in mourning. When they showed up, and all the ladies were dressed in white, they looked like little dolls. My brother, who has a wrangler sense of humor, said, "I want one of *them*!"

It was strange for me to be in the middle of this juncture of people. Nobody on the cathedral staff knew who Dave was. They were astonished that 500 people showed up at the funeral. When our friend was up there in the pulpit to read Dave's accomplishments from the obituary, the church staff looked at each other, "Who was this guy?!" Our priest from Sedona officiated, and she was down-to-earth and from her heart, which Dave always loved about her.

We picked out beautiful hymns, some of Dave's favorites. The cathedral does not allow you to have any kind of music you want. We had to stay with traditional hymns. I was a little sad about this because I had wanted someone to sing, "Wind Beneath My Wings," since Dave *was* that for all of us—the wind beneath our wings.

On the way home from Phoenix after the funeral, we had a flat tire. We were stuck at a tire shop for hours and didn't get home until very late that night. Truly, after all that I'd been through the previous few months, I felt like I had "no air left" in my tires.

We all have dark places in our life that we have to go through. In those months after Dave died, I was in a dark haze, a nothingness and numbness. I not only lost my teacher; I lost my husband. It was very hard to go on after that. And then, of course, I had Veritas Publishing to run. How was I going to get back into the swing of that without him? I just didn't know. I couldn't make decisions or do much of anything for a while. He had told me to give myself time. He said that whatever I needed would be there for me.

Eventually, I pulled out of it. As I write this now, it has been ten years since he passed. I know he would be very happy with what I've done with his work and that there are so many of you whose lives have been transformed. He left me as the steward of his work because he knew it needed to be watched over and established correctly for perpetuity. If I hadn't had that strong purpose of the work we shared together, I don't know if I would have pulled out of the grief of losing him. His Spirit lives on in the teachings, and by tending to those, I am always with him.

A couple of years ago, I was in Canada with some of our students. We were talking about how we all carry a light inside. You may have heard the song, "This little light of mine, I'm gonna let it shine." We all have that spiritual light inside of us, and it takes just one spark to ignite it. One of the women said, "That moment happened to me when I came across *Power vs. Force*. It compelled me. I had to finish reading the book no matter what it took." When that door opens, you can't shut it again. We experience it and love it and nourish it, and then we share it with other people. That's our quest in life, to let our little light shine. Dave did it in his way, and he ignited our inner light. I'm doing it in my way, and you are doing it in your way. Together, we are "the light of the world."

Questions and Answers

Q: You must miss him terribly.
A: I do miss him, but it's not a hurtful miss, because I know he is happy with what we're doing.

Q: What were his last words?
A: "Bye-bye! See you soon!" *Laughter...* Dave had a funny sense of humor. He would be laughing with us at that joke. Well, we knew that he was going to pass soon, but we didn't know when. I asked him, "How do I handle all of this work that you left me with?" And he said, "Oh Suzie, just use your common sense." That's one of the last things he said to me.

Q: Did anyone look for relics when his body was cremated?
A: I won't say yes. And I won't say no. But I will say that I have the majority of his ashes at home. The Columbarium at our local Episcopal church has some of them. They have the niche that they put the ashes of their members into. Dave wanted a wooden box. He loved wood and he didn't want a fancy urn.

Q: Can anyone go to the Columbarium and visit Doc's ashes?
A: It is church property, and it is locked. You need to check with the church office to find out the times that it's open. It's important to be respectful of the church's Christian customs and the fact that many people are there, not just Doc. They can't accommodate long visits or rituals. At the ranch, it's different. For example, when our Hindu friend Swamiji came from India to pay his respect to

Dave at the house, I brought out the box of Dave's ashes, and he was able to express his ritual in the Hindu custom. Swamiji said he recognized Dave as a very high being. Swamiji is a wise spiritual teacher. He said that it's extremely rare that you find someone like David, born in the Western world, who also understands Eastern religions.

Dave and I talked one time about going to India. He said, "I can't go to India because I'll go to the Ganges, sit on the river bank and die. I will not come back. I will leave the body there. I can remember several lifetimes, and that's what I did." So, he had been in some kind of religious order or whatever in India and he had great respect for that. He had respect for all religions.

Q: What was that like, dealing with the time leading up to his passing and grappling with the loss of him?
A: He told me to wait three days before cremating his body, and so we didn't cremate it for three days. I could feel the presence in the house. He was still there. It was like he hadn't even gone. And then when we cremated the body, that's when it hit me, that he is gone. I could feel that he had left the planet. And that's when I went into kind of a shock. I just sat in front of the TV and didn't know what I was even watching—just things moving on the screen. I'd go out to the office and the staff were playing his lecture videos because they were working on our lecture products. And that was the hardest part—to hear his voice. A few years later, I myself often did the work of listening to the lecture videos to make sure they were ready to ship to the people who purchased them. While Dave was alive, we had several volunteers who did this for us, but they left after he passed. We are short-handed, so I fill in to do things like that. I'm glad I can listen to his lectures now and not go into grief. Recently, we shifted to offering the lecture videos on a streaming service and that's a lot easier than duplicating and shipping the discs.

After he passed, for the first three months, I went into a shell and couldn't do anything. And then, all of a sudden, it was okay, and after that, it was a year, another year, and so on. Now it has been ten years. It's difficult to come back into life, after you had that much blessed time with someone, whether they are enlightened or not, it doesn't matter. It's hard to go through that loss. First of all, he was David to me. He was the love of my life, my husband and my partner in everything. And second, he was my spiritual teacher, as well as everyone else's spiritual teacher. So that part was the hardest, because I felt like I lost not only the love of my life, but also the spiritual teacher of my life.

Some people want to run out right away and find another spiritual guide, but you don't need to. He left a whole embodiment of work for us to practice and learn from. We can read, listen, and watch all the material that he left us. It's there for us. A lot of people think, "Oh, he's no longer teaching," but that is not true. He left us so much information in his seminars, and in his work, that even now I go back and learn something new every time I listen to him. Every time I read a book, I find that something else opens up to me, even though I've read it before. If I go back and read it again, I see something in a different light. Probably you've had that experience too. It's not only information, but also the Presence that came through David.

He never left anyone to teach the work, because he completed it himself. There are many people out there who want to teach his work, and claim to represent it, but they change it to suit themselves and there's not that same Presence. And I want to stress this—Dave did not give permission for anyone to teach his work. He is the teacher of his work. He left all these lectures for you to see him and understand who he was. So, I'm saying that *he is still teaching*, even though he left the body. His teachings help us understand mankind and understand the workings of the world. World crises come and go. His teachings are always relevant to help us.

Q: What would Doc want to tell us right now?
A: Interesting you should ask that. The other day at three o'clock in the morning, I woke up and the answer to that question is what

came to me. It's what I felt Dave was wanting people to know. And that is: The only thing you take into the life hereafter, and the only thing that really matters, is your soul. This is the only thing that comes in with us when we're born, and the only thing that goes out with us when our life on earth ends. So that means we are responsible for our own spirituality. Are we nourishing our soul? That's what matters in life. Too often, people spend all their time feeding the ego, not the soul! Our soul is actually the only thing we're responsible for in our life. So, I think what Dave would want me to say is to tell people that they are responsible for their own soul, and to not lose sight of that in the endless distractions of this world.

Dave left us this huge body of work, and the body of work answers every question. All we have to do is watch his videos and listen to his audios, with an open heart and the willingness to do our inner work and be changed. People say it's hard to do the soul work. I'm the same way. We work all day long doing things for our family and jobs—how will we have time to work on our soul? Still, if there's anything I've learned from his teaching, it's that everybody is responsible for their own soul. We have our great teacher, but even he cannot do it for us. It's up to us to prioritize our soul.

STEWARDSHIP OF THE WORK

Dave's passing brought home to me the fact that our time on earth is limited. How are we spending the time we have left? Do we spend time with our inner Self? Dave gave us the example of prioritizing time for inner work. He was always challenging himself to take that next step in his awareness. He did it out of love for God and mankind. He didn't do it to "prove" something or "get" somewhere on the Map! He did it for the sake of *Gloria in Excelsis Deo*—for the Glory of God in the Highest.

Big leaps are sudden, but they take time to integrate into our being. Dave had a very high experience when he was younger, and then it took him thirty years after that to develop the framework of understanding that he had when he started giving his lectures. An experience that happened in a flash of time, took him three decades to incorporate into his being!

He didn't begin teaching and writing spiritual books until he was in his late sixties. After *Power vs. Force* came out in 1995, he became a prolific writer. He wrote three books and said, "I'm done," but he ended up writing many more after that! He was responding to the questions people had, and he was expressing his own evolving inner awareness. He was thinking of every aspect and every scenario in life where people would have questions. He challenged himself to present the material in different ways, because some people are visual, some people are auditory, and some people are feeling.

He knew he didn't have much time left, so he made use of every day, to improve himself and to help us improve ourselves. He did more in his last year of life than many people do in a lifetime. No one knows how much time they have left here. That's something I think about every day. I live and breathe the work. A friend of mine says to me, "Susan you are working around the clock, 24/7. Even at night, you're thinking about Doc's work and what you need to do for it!" It's true. I shared this commitment with David, that, with whatever time I have left, my life was given to the work that we established.

Being the Steward

I want to thank all of you for your love of the work. If you are reading this book, you are interested in David and the work that he left for us. Maybe you are finding it after I have left the planet. I hope this chapter gives you an understanding of what we've done so that seekers far into the future will find these teachings when they are ready for it.

At our most recent gathering, in 2019, before the Covid-19 pandemic shut down events and traveling, many of you came from far away, even from across the world, to be together and to pay your respect to Dave's work. Whenever we have our gatherings, it makes my heart full to see all of you there. I find it very encouraging to be with you and to hear your appreciation for the teachings. Thank you for sharing how his work has helped you. We were doing the events once a year until the pandemic forced us to cancel the event in 2020. Now it's 2022, and the powers-that-be are still expressing caution about large indoor gatherings. So, we have shifted to regular virtual gatherings. Life is always evolving. It's wonderful to see you in the virtual event and to have a chance to address your questions.

After Dave passed, it was hard for me to get back out there to do events without him. We were always on stage together. But he and I knew that's how it had to be. I had to be left behind to oversee his body of work, the ranch where he lived, and the Institute he established.

Some of our people have struggled because they were attached to Dave as a person. They like having the teacher in a physical form. Dave told me it would happen: "People want a teacher in physical form. After I'm gone, they will go off to see someone else." It's hard for me to understand why people are so attached to Dave's personality. He never made it about him as a person; it was always about the teachings themselves.

David was not a proponent of channeling, as you probably know from his writings. I do not "channel" him. He said specifically that *no one* would channel him, and if they claim to, do not believe them!

It's more simply that I can express what his wishes might be. He trained me as the steward of his work, and I try to live by the standards that he taught me. I'm not an expert. Who is? Dave himself did not claim to be an expert. I try to do the very best I can with what I've been given to do. I fall flat on my face sometimes, but I don't live there! In other words, I recognize my faults, and I work hard to overcome them and not continue in them. As Dave said, the path of Truth is a razor's edge. We all know what we should be doing, and sometimes we go against that. So, then, that's karma, isn't it? If we're lucky, karma comes up and gives us a Zen whack to get us back on the straight and narrow. Some people, I notice, are not so fortunate; they get lost in spiritual fantasy without realizing it.

I'm in a role right now that I'll probably be in for the rest of my lifetime. If you had told me that this is what my life would be, I would have said, "No way, that's not what I want for myself." I thought I might get to retire one day, but now I see that's not possible. That's what I mean by time. Over time, I've come to embrace my life as it has turned out to be. I'm happy to do this work as long as I can.

I will share with you something that might surprise you. We'd like to think that our society has evolved to a point where people are respectful, regardless of gender. But not so! I find that when you're a woman in a stewardship role, people question you and doubt you more often. Dave was a man. It is challenging that the responsibility of stewardship rests on me. If I were a man saying the same things, people would fulfill the request without talking back. Or they'd say, "Oh okay, I don't see it that way, but I respect what you're telling me." When you're a woman doing it, they often don't like to hear it from you. They demand to know, "Well, how do *you* know that?" Or they'll say, "Oh no, I disagree. I think it should be done this other way." Or, "Are you sure that's what Doc wanted?" That last complaint is especially surprising. People who were around Dave for a fraction of the time think they know better what he wanted than I do, as the one he entrusted! I lived with Dave and was trained by Dave. He and I discussed in detail what he wished for his body of work. And, also, on a spiritual level, he told me I have within my aura what he wants me to do. I think it's safe to say I have trustworthy knowledge of what his wishes were. I also have the total commitment to seeing it through.

Since Dave's passing, the work has continued to touch people's lives. New people come into it every day. They write to us and tell us how their lives have changed, and that makes me very happy. That's the reason I'm still doing this. Dave's books are going overseas more and more, and so we are getting new requests for the foreign rights to translate his books. As it continues to grow, I see that this is my role until I die. This is what Dave wanted of me. He worked into his 80s, and it looks like I will be too. It makes me feel fulfilled that I can keep his work alive and be here for the people that it touches. I appreciate all of you who support our efforts with your love and prayers and contributions.

I am not what Dave was. If God had wanted two of him, then it would have been that way. Yet I am what I am, and somebody was needed to do what I do, so that Dave could do what he had to do. I accept that I was put into this role to bring whatever I could bring to it, just like you are bringing whatever you are to the role that life has given you. Each of us is where we are meant to be.

I know that some people expect me to step in and be Dave, but I'm not Dave. No one can teach the work like that. All I can do is give you what he has left for us. That's my job. I can't teach it. I'm not a great public speaker. I'm not a well-known author. Dave was all of those things, and he left me to be the steward of his work. Dave's books and teachings are left in my care, and it's my responsibility to keep them as pure as possible, which means to make sure they stay aligned with Truth and do not get caught in webs of distortion.

Stewardship of the Teachings

Now I will share with you the most challenging part of my role on a daily basis. I hope by sharing Dave's wishes that you will have a better understanding of how you can join us in being a good steward of his teachings so that they remain as pure as possible for future generations.

Dave put me in charge of keeping his work as pure as possible, which means preserving it as direct from him, protected from other people's influences. He made it clear that he did not want anyone teaching his work because it is pure in itself. If someone else teaches the work, then it's no longer his pure work. He had a rare Realization that we will probably never have. Why would someone want to mess that up and try to explain or teach about it? It just doesn't make any sense. His work doesn't need to be "helped" or "explained." Dave always said, the work will get out there, "by word of mouth." We don't need to push it! It will get out there on its own, and it will go where it needs to go when the time is ready for it to go there.

Dave was extremely advanced in his teachings. He did not want others to put the Map of Consciousness® in their books or videos or websites because he knew they could not give the context for it. Their ego would distort it. He was so discouraged by what people's egos did with the Map of Consciousness® that he told one of our friends, "I'm sorry I ever shared the Map!"

Can you imagine if the Map were not trademarked? It would be used to market all kinds of products and services. "Slippers that raise your calibration to 540." "Annuities that calibrate the highest." Dave knew that would happen, and so that's why he was very clear to say "No" to all requests for reproducing or disseminating the Map.

According to the law, the Map of Consciousness® cannot be reproduced or altered because it is copyrighted and trademarked. That means it cannot be put into your book or your video or your presentation, just because you like it. This is true for any quote, photograph, or piece of art. You have to get the permission of the author or creator of that work in order to put it into something of yours. I have a friend who wrote a book that included a photograph and some quotations from Mother Teresa. She had to get special written permission from the Mother Teresa Center in Rome for every word she quoted and to print the photo of Mother Teresa in her book. She was happy to do that, out of respect for Mother Teresa and her foundation.

If you are excited about the Map of Consciousness® and want to share it, then it is best simply to refer people directly to Dave's work. They will understand it better if they get it straight from his carrier wave. Why not point people directly to the source? Why would you want to put it in *your* book, website, video or whatever? If you want to write a book or make a video, why not simply do what David did—go into your own unique experiences and share about *that*? Share from your *own* ideas and creativity. This is much more truthful than taking someone else's creative and spiritual work and trying to reproduce or explain it.

Distortions occur when people try to teach Dave's work. Many people out there think they should be allowed to teach his work, but no one is capable of teaching his work. For example, he created his teaching on "surrender" out of what *he* was. How could anyone else come close to that depth of surrender and say, "Here's what he meant by surrender"? He created "devotional nonduality" out of what *he* was. How could anyone else come close to what he embodied of devotion and nonduality, let alone speak about it? He told us over and over again that you cannot teach something unless you *are* it.

Some people are playing the part. They wear white robes or something like that, gaze into your eyes, and so forth. They take on the persona of a "spiritual teacher" or "master" or "guru," and amazingly, many Doc students fall for it. One time, I ran into someone who was from Sedona. He wrote a book that is well-known. We were in the Post Office, and he was mailing something. He was dressed in white robes and such. He kept smiling at me, and I thought, *Who is this guy?* He said to me, "Hi, I'm so and so." I didn't know who he was until he told me his name, and then I recognized he was a popular author. He was playing the part of a spiritual teacher and spiritual author.

Dave did not play any part. He was 100% genuine. He did not want to be regarded as a guru or avatar, and he was never interested in having followers. He just wanted to be called a "sharer" or "teacher," because that's what he was. He was sharing with us his experience of all the levels of consciousness. His work stands on its own. When people try to "teach" his work, they are putting *their* slant on it and then it gets distorted.

There are plenty of wanna-be teachers out there. They encounter Dave's work and then they want to publish a book about it, or they put up videos in which they talk about spiritual work and they have his photograph in the background, hoping to give the impression that Dave is somehow approving of them, which he is not!

Every week, someone writes us to say, "I want to put the Map of Consciousness® in my book, video, conference presentation," or whatever. When we say it is not legal, some of them get angry! They become hostile because they are not allowed to use his material in whatever way they want. All we did was say, "No, the Map is trademarked by Dr. Hawkins, and therefore it cannot be reproduced in your work."

Dave was very explicit about that. He directed us not to let other people publish or disseminate the Map of Consciousness®

in any way, because they will put their own slant on it, and fifty years from now, who will know what he really meant? That's why he did not appoint a teacher of his work. He did not want someone to put their slant on his body of work. He is the only teacher and author of his work. If someone implies that they have his blessing to use his Map of Consciousness®, or to teach his work, or to explain it, they are not telling the truth. They do not have that blessing or permission from him.

People are not aware when their ego is talking. They say, "Oh, Doc wouldn't mind if I did this, because I am promoting his work," when actually it is their own *self*-promotion, but they can't see it. Or, they say, "Well, I believe that Doc was thinking this or that when he said this," and they give their opinion that changes the meaning of what he said. Or, they write to us, saying, "Oh, yes, but I am the exception to the rule. What I'm doing really helps you." The egotism comes through loud and clear, doesn't it? But it's unconscious, so they do not recognize it in themselves. If you want to be a good steward of Dave's teachings, then make sure you are not using him for your own personal gain.

Even people who criticize Dave and his work like to put up his Map of Consciousness® or use his name on their website, because it draws visitors to their website and then they make money from the visitor clicks. You see what I'm saying? Even the critics like to refer to Dave and have his Map on their website so they can manipulate traffic on the internet to benefit their own pockets. Criticism attracts curiosity. Negativity sells.

Other people take the Map of Consciousness® and alter it to what they want, maybe with different colors or different design. Perhaps they think if they tweak it, then they can put their stamp of claim on it. In one case, which is so flagrant it's funny, a "leadership" website posted the Map of Consciousness® but removed the "God" column! They had their company brand all over the page to give the impression that this was their material. I wonder how far they'll get now that they've taken God out of everything!

I understand the enthusiasm. People get excited about his work, and they jump on the bandwagon of, "Everyone needs to read this or hear this! It is life-changing!" And they imagine they will "help" Dave's work by posting his teachings and video clips everywhere. Or they put up videos of themselves on the internet talking about him or his work. This goes against what Dave taught. He told us to focus on our own consciousness, not "saving the world." The *real* point of his teaching is not to make sure that it gets "everywhere," but to make sure that it enters your own heart. *That's* what helps mankind—when your own heart is truly transformed. And that takes constant devotion to your inner work. It has nothing to do with posting, promoting, blogging, and disseminating to others.

David also did not want people setting up centers or organizations using his name, or using names that he coined such as "Devotional Nonduality." When he was alive, we had to close down a group of Doc students who had set up a center in Sedona and were doing retreats based on his work. They had his picture on an altar. Dave said the problem was that they were subtly setting themselves up as teachers of his work, and there was no way they could ever be teachers of his work. They did not have the inner realizations that the teachings were based on, so they were misleading people. Doc students were signing up and staying at these "retreats" because they were led to believe that Doc approved it, due to proximity. Doc students were also making large donations to this center, believing it had Dave's approval. Dave had to make clear that he did not approve of what they were doing, and he asked them to cease and desist immediately. A similar problem has occurred in Sedona since he passed away. Please use discernment.

Spiritual Responsibility

Dave did his work for the love of mankind, not for himself. When you love something, you protect it. In this world, in order to protect the veracity of a teaching, you have to copyright it as intellectual property. Dave was pragmatic in how he wanted his work

established. It is spiritual work, but it also has to exist on this earthly plane. He respected both the spiritual and the earthly levels of
reality.

When you are responsible for things that you love or that you
want to take care of, you protect them. That's true of your home,
your family, your children, your car, your devices, isn't it? That's
how it works here in the earthly domain. If someone helps themselves to one of these things, without your permission, you take
steps to protect it. Especially you do that when it is very precious
to you and you love it. I hope you will join us in our responsibility
to honor David's wishes for the purity of his work.

We are especially concerned to keep Dave's work pure for the
people who never had the chance to see him when he was alive.
If you watch and listen to his lectures, then you are learning from
the same events that we went to and learned from. Dave is not
dead; he has just changed form. His physical body is gone, but his
body of work remains, and his energy is in that body of work. All
you have to do is read it or listen to it or live it, and you are right
there with him. He's not here in the flesh and bone, but he *is* here
in the Spirit. He told us that he would continue to be here and be
available as a vibration within the collective consciousness. He also
said that if you focus on his energy in your mind and heart, then
he is present with you. I find that to be very true. Whenever I need
him, he is here.

Some followers have become fundamentalist with his teachings, and I cannot understand this except that it must be human
nature to get dogmatic. For example, they will only listen to music
or read books that calibrate at a very high level. Let's remember
that Dave loved country-western music! He told us that as long
as something calibrates over 200, it is beneficial. "Higher" does
not mean "better." Everything has its own context. Dave taught
us not to mix levels. He taught us to have common sense. For instance, when that pilot told us to prepare for a crash landing into
Albuquerque, we were glad he wasn't listening to an OM Chant!
He was on task with what he had to do in the moment. There's a

time and place for everything. Dave taught us to strive to be *ordinary*, not stick out like a sore thumb trying to "be spiritual."

Someone recounted a strange experience. They went to a get-together of Doc students in Sedona. It was their first time to meet up with a group of Doc students, and they were eager for the opportunity. This is part of human nature; we all long for fellowship and a place to belong. When they arrived at the front door, they introduced themselves by using their name, "Hi, nice to meet you, my name is so-and-so." The students who met them at the door said, "Oh, no, we don't use personal names here. That name is not who we really are." This is taking Dave's work too literally! It is mixing levels. David never used his spiritual teaching to put a barrier between himself and others. When he was with others, he was as natural as he could be. He was the only person I've ever known who was truly beyond a personal name, but he still referred to himself by his name and allowed others to call him by his name!

Other people take the work and twist it into aims that it was never intended for. Recently, someone sent us websites where stock investors were using kinesiology and the Map of Consciousness® to do investments. They claimed to use kinesiology to increase your investment gain! Wasn't Dave as clear as day on that? He said you cannot use muscle-testing or the Map for any kind of financial or personal gain. He and I never used muscle-testing on investments or anything related to personal concerns like that. We were very good at the arm, but we never used it for personal gain. Why? Because we knew the answers would not be accurate. The consciousness calibration method simply does not work when you are hoping to get something out of it, or when you have a personal agenda.

Unbelievably, there are people who charge money for calibrations. They have Dave's picture or his name on their website or his terminology like "consciousness calibration," so that Doc students are led to believe that the website is connected to his work. But it's a scam. The intention is to lure curious Doc students and get their money. Why would you pay someone to do calibrations?

Why would you pay money to subscribe to a website that promises calibrations? What makes you believe their calibrations would even be accurate? It is a hook to the ego, to curiosity, to naiveté. What they want is your money. Some of them are notorious frauds who have repeatedly evaded capture. Even if we wanted to shut down their website, we can't because of the fact that they have no central address; they live in motorhomes or otherwise go from place to place to evade the law. At little cost to them, they have created websites that appear very convincing in order to make money from seekers' curiosity.

Discernment is part and parcel of spiritual responsibility. When Dave talked about "the wolf in sheep's clothing," you need to know this is an actual phenomenon that occurs everywhere, even within the Doc community. You think they are sincere, but they want money to calibrate things for you, heal you, help you get enlightened, give you a treatment, reach the 500s+, or whatever their pick-up line is. You don't need someone else to tell you what you need to "raise" your level or to "heal" you. You already know what you need to work on, don't you? You just have to do it! You don't need to pay people to do calibrations for you. You don't need to know the latest calibrations of this or that. You have the answers you need already inside of you—if you are willing to spend the time to do the inner work to uncover them. Dave and I did thousands of published calibrations that are there for everyone to study and learn from.

Some people use Dave's name or their association to him for personal gain—renting out rooms or houses, and getting clients for past life regressions, treatments, retreats, etc. Would they have any renters or clients if they weren't referring to Doc? They are drawing their business from Doc students who are led to believe there is a special connection to Doc, or a special effect from being close to where he lived, when there is not. It is misleading.

Dave told me he was glad that the place in Wisconsin where he had his snowbank experience was never pinpointed. Otherwise, there would be people hawking Doc trinkets or setting up signs for vacation rentals and retreat rooms "near the holy snowbank where Doc dissolved into Infinite Love!"

He warned us about the hooks of specialness and greed. If your past life regressions tell you that you were some famous incredible saint, apostle, or high-calibrating person, you might want to take it with a grain of salt. Dave liked to point out that he was a slave, a pirate, and a blacksmith in other lifetimes.

Just because someone got to be with Dave in person doesn't make them special. I was with him all the time, but I am not special. I just have a certain role to fulfill, and let me tell you, it can be challenging! There is no hierarchy of specialness in this path. Just because someone lives in Sedona or attended the satsangs or lectures in person doesn't make them any more knowledgeable than anyone else. We all come to Dave's teachings at the perfect time and in the perfect way that we are meant to. We will receive what we are supposed to receive out of the teachings if we are humble and come from the heart.

Some people are very gracious when we request them to stop referencing him in a misleading way or to take down their illegal use of Dave's work. They respect Dave and his teachings, and they simply did not realize what they were doing. Thank you! Other people don't like to be called out on their misuses. Dave told me I would have to have a thick skin, and he was right. I try not to lose my faith in mankind. Mainly, I am baffled that people who claim to "love" the work give us such a hard time in our responsibility to preserve its integrity.

I would like to say, "Everything runs very smoothly here," but it doesn't always. This earthly realm is not paradise. Human nature is not always kind. We have many outside pressures, just like when you're in a family, and you have teenagers, or you have little ones that are constantly demanding your attention. It's the same thing with running an organization. One of my challenges is to deal with negative responses, and to present our shared goal in such a way that people understand that they have a role to help us do the very best we can to keep Dave's material aligned with truth, so that long after we're all gone, the people who need it will find it, in its *pristine state*.

I hope that, by sharing David's wishes for the stewardship of his teachings, I have helped you understand our shared responsibility to honor his work. There are times I get so frustrated that I think, *I just can't do this one more day!* Then, something wonderful happens. I get a letter from someone saying that David's work changed their life, and I realize that it's all worth it. His work is a great gift to all of us, now and in the future. I hope you will join us in our stewardship to keep it pure.

We each have stewardship of our soul. In addition to stewardship of the teachings, we have stewardship of our own inner life. We cannot pass it off to someone else. We are responsible for our own spiritual quest, whom we pick as a teacher, and whom we pick as friends. It's up to us to choose the spiritual influences that we follow, and to follow them in a sincere way.

A few years ago, a friend invited me to attend Mother Teresa's canonization for sainthood. It was in St. Peter's Square at the Vatican, and we had the opportunity to see and hear Pope Francis, who did the ceremony. He is truly a beautiful person, in spirit and body. He gave an uplifting message about compassion. I think that the Catholic Church has a very good leader in him as the Pope. A friend also invited me to hear the 17th Karmapa, a very good leader and teacher of compassion in the Buddhist tradition. It is a great blessing to have teachers like this.

Still, no one can take you there. Even if you are in a great church or a great spiritual group, even if you have the best teacher, it's still up to you to make the effort and to have a pure heart. Dave said, "Straight and narrow is the path; waste no time." And now we're back to where we started this chapter: time. Maybe we have less of it than we think we do. Let's focus on the things that matter.

What I would like to see more of in our group is basic kindness to other people. Each one of us is the "light of the world," and it's up to us to show that light and to nurture our soul, which is light. The only thing we take with us when we pass from this world is our soul, so we need to nourish it in ourselves and in others. We can do that through kindness.

Questions and Answers

Q: I love that Doc was a pragmatist. "Just be kind for God's sakes!" he said.

A: Once you start being kind, it's hard to go back. And when something happens that isn't kind, it might be hard to accept that. We have a quote in the office that says, "For every action, there is a reaction." And sometimes it's a negative reaction. We are all the lightning rods in which our message is passed through to the world around us, and to the people around us. And, so, each one of us is like a little flame that can light up the world and other people. If we can remember that and pass along something kind, Doc would be proud of us.

Recently, at our annual event, I saw so many people do kind things for each other. It was really amazing to be around that kind of energy. It doesn't matter if you're going to be five minutes late for something, and who cares if you lose your seat near the front row?! Take the time to help someone. Whether it's crossing the street or soothing a child or playing with an animal, everybody has their own ability to help make the world a better place. This is what Dave said. To raise each ship is impossible, but if you raise the level of the sea, the ships will all be raised up together. That's how we can make the world a better place for everybody to live in, if we use kindness as a tool in our everyday life. It will make us a better person and also create a better world to live in.

Q: What do you see as some of the problems within the Doc community?

A: The problems can probably be summed up in two words: "Spiritual ego." It just floors me when people say or think, "Well, I'm in the 500s." They are looking down on others. How do you know that's where you're at? If you're saying it or thinking it, you probably aren't it! It's very hard for me to understand why people would think they're better than someone else or use the Map of Consciousness® in that way to think they're "higher" than others—it's just beyond my comprehension! People don't seem to notice that their spiritual ego will jump in and take over, and then they think they are holier, more pious, more moral, more correct, more knowledgeable about Doc, or whatever the superiority is. I will never understand that.

I've experienced that attitude not only in our group, but also in the churches that believe, "We do it right, they do it wrong." We all need a little more humility! We need to realize that it was a blessing even to encounter Doc's work. We were blessed to have been in his presence and even to hear his teachings, which will get us through the hard times in life. We need to be there for each other, not judge each other.

I've heard that some of our study groups get a bit heady and dogmatic. It's fine to study and discuss and share information. Just make sure to keep the ego out of it. It's not about knowing everything he ever wrote or said. It's not about literalism of every word or quoting chapter and verse. If you've read all of Doc's books and you can quote them for every occasion, good for you! Just remember this doesn't mean you're holier or more knowledgeable than others; it might just mean you have a good memory!

Are you able to listen with your heart? That's what matters. Are you humble? That's the cornerstone. Are you putting one of his teachings into practice every day, without exception? That's what works. "Constancy" he called it. It's not enough to know it in your head. His words have to go into your being and your soul. Dave taught us that our spiritual path begins with humility and kindness.

Q: Aren't the 500s better than the 400s?
A: No. That's the ego's perception. No level is better than another. It's just what it is. So many people think that you have to be higher on those levels, yet you don't have to be! You don't have to be anything but what you are! This is where God wants you to

be. Why would you try to be something you are not? Until you've mastered where you are, how will you be taken to another level?

Between the 400s to 500s is where all the action is. If you're in the higher 500s, it's virtually impossible to function. Our world wouldn't function if there were a lot of people that high. It's a small minority. People think that in the 500s they're supposed to walk around in a white robe, think only beautiful thoughts, and wear a never-ending beatific smile on their face. I'm here to tell you that it's not about leaving fairy dust in your trail. Dave wasn't fooled by that fairy dust sparkle, and I guess I'm not either.

In my own experience, we go up and down. Sometimes I think I'm at one level, then something happens and I answer at a lower level, or I think about it at another level ... like how I'd like to slam the door in someone's face when they are rude! *Laughter*... I loved about Dave that I could walk in the house after a hard day of dealing with problems, and I could b***h about it, and then he'd make a joke and get me laughing. He'd empathize and let me vent, and then he'd say something funny about it all and we'd end up laughing the night away. He never judged the "low"—he just laughed you out of it. We all have our low times and our high times. If we judge the low, then we'll never be given the high.

Sometimes we find ourselves in the lower numbers on the Map of Consciousness®; we're down in depression, grief or whatever. That's why I say you can't live at a certain number all the time on the Map. Have you noticed how you're sailing along, feeling great, and then something comes up in your life that throws you down into the lower levels for a while, such as grief, jealousy, fear, or whatever it may be?

It's a challenge for all of us to live our life like Doc would want us to. He would want us to do the work by supporting each other. If there's someone in the group who is having problems, help them, because that's what groups are for. We're meant to care for each other in times of need. We're there to hold each other up, because there's a common denominator that runs through all of us and connects all of us. We can help each other laugh out of the "lows," instead of thinking we're superior.

Q: How do I let go of wanting to "get to a higher number"?
A: Just forget the numbers. The Map of Consciousness® is a tool and not a measuring stick. All you need to know is: What are you currently working on to improve in yourself? And, usually, life itself brings this up. Whatever struggle or uncertainty or conflict or grit is going on in your life, then that's your work. Life is your greatest teacher. Dave said that. It's not really about the calibrations or where you are on the chart. Stop obsessing about that. You subconsciously already know about where you are and what you'd like to overcome.

Dave was extraordinary. He worked nonstop to delve into every aspect and angle of experience, from the lowest to the highest. He was a recluse and went into his inner Self so deeply. He put the time in to explore every level of consciousness. That's why he was able to help so many different people on so many different levels.

People want someone else to take them to a higher level. He gave you the Map, but you need to do the work on your own. Each of us knows, deep inside, something we can let go of or something we can step into. Whatever that next step is: Will we do it? That's the question. I don't know if any of us are willing to go into our inner Self like he did. He literally left everything and everyone in order to focus there. I don't think I could do that. I'm not called to that like he was. He spent a lot of time by himself. This would be a very lonely existence for most people.

Q: How can I lessen the grip of the spiritual ego?
A: You could try to curb any need to be special and be recognized. I had a friend here at the ranch and we were noticing the ducks. We have several ducks on our pond. She asked why the male ducks are colorful and flashy, while the female ducks are plain. I told her that the male ducks are colorful and flashy because they have to stand out if a predator comes. The female ducks are very plain and brown because when they sit on the eggs, they have to be

hidden. The male ducks go around and flash their colors to draw attention to themselves so the predators will notice them and not the nest. Sometimes the male ducks give their lives for the female duck to be protected. I was telling her, "Yeah, sometimes it's not very good to be all shiny and bright and showing off—it might be the end of you!"

And that's what Doc said too. You don't have to be the one out-front. You don't have to be the big shot who knows every-thing, the one who stands out, the one who is special. You can go behind the scenes and do three times the work, three times as fast. The problem is that the ego wants recognition. "Look at me. Look what *I* did." But, in reality, it's better to do your task and let it go. Dave told me, "Just do the good and let it go." Can you do some-thing kind without needing a reward or recognition? People want the karmic merit for doing something good. Probably if you're doing it to get the merit, you just cancelled getting the merit!

The other day I was in town and went into a restaurant to get lunch. There was a homeless man outside the restaurant who said he was hungry, so I bought a hamburger and gave it to him when I walked out. Well, guess what? He fed it to his dog. So, I got to let go of expecting my generosity to go a certain way. If we give something, it might go entirely differently than what we intended it to be. That's what Dave meant when he said, "We plant the seeds but let go of the results." It's good when we can do our jobs or our work around the house or in society and not need to be in the limelight with it. Or get a reward for it. Dave did all that he did, not for any reward, except the fulfillment of knowing he had done his part to help mankind.

Q: How did he, and both of you, handle trials such as his work being attacked?
A: He always said, "Just let it go." Someone has written negative things about Dave. It was hard to let go at first, because we trust-ed that person at one time. But things change. Intentions change. And we have to accept that there are always critical people out

there, and they like to see the worst in you—and even make money from criticizing you. Dave said, "Let it go. It's a flash in the pan." Dave didn't like it. I mean, nobody would like someone insinuating negative things about you or your work. But Dave viewed it from the perspective that those sorts of people are not integrous. If they were, they would simply say, "I disagree with you, but that's okay," and then they'd go on to something else that they thought was better for them. I mean, if you really believe something is false, then why write books on it? It must be that you're getting something out of it. Dave accepted that some people are going to be negative and greedy for money or fame. Dave thought it best to surrender them to karma. A friend asked him, "Can I pray for that person who betrayed you?" Dave said, "No. It's best to surrender him to God." When it happened, Dave wrote a clarification about it to his students. He felt a responsibility to do that because people were confused and writing to ask us about it. Other than that one clarifying email to his students, he let it go.

Q: Why don't you put all of Doc's lectures on digital download?
A: We just recently made all the lectures available on a streaming service, which you can subscribe to on our website for a minimal fee. Each lecture lasted about six hours, and we have about 200 of his lectures. Do you realize how much material that is?! That's why it took a while for us to get it all up on the internet. Our staff is busy working on multiple projects, but over the last few years, they were able to digitalize the material and upload it into a user-friendly streaming service for you.

Q: Why don't you make all the teachings available for free?
A: If Doc had wanted to give his teachings away for free, he would have done that. Instead, he established Veritas Publishing and his Institute as the legal owners of the material, and he wanted it all to be copyright-protected and his Map of Consciousness® trademarked as unique intellectual property. Stewardship of his teachings was very important to him. Look at how careful he was

in testing every sentence that he said and wrote!

Doc did not charge for his spiritual teachings. He said they were a gift to him, and he shared them out of gratitude.

But he also recognized that spiritual organizations have a responsibility to charge reasonable fees to cover their costs of production and operation. This is just common sense. There is the fantasy that spiritual materials should not have a cost to them. Doc did not teach us that. It's mixing levels. It's being naive. Doc was pragmatic. Do you have any idea how much it costs us just to keep the office running with computers, internet services, utilities, insurances, legal fees, software programs, staff compensation, preparing and printing books, producing videos, and that is just the beginning! We'd have to close down the office if we did not have revenue from our books and streaming services. Since Dave's passing, the internet has exploded with "free" PDF downloads of our books, and people putting up YouTubes with "free" audiobooks of our books. This is stealing. Maybe they mean well, I don't know. But they would do well to understand that each "free" download hurts the very organization that published the work, and that Doc himself established. They say, "Oh we're helping get the word out." Actually, it dilutes and takes away from the work.

People tell me, "If Doc's material was free on the internet, then more people could find it." Doc was never interested in wide dissemination. His approach was the exact opposite of that! He said he wanted his books to spread "by word of mouth." He knew that people would find the work when they were ready for it. Dave and I thought things through into the future, far beyond our own generations alive today. He wanted his work to be self-sustaining and as pure as possible. Putting up free material on the internet hurts both of those intentions. So please look down the line. How does it help the work when you undermine the organization that made it available to you? Think about it before you see something that you can get "for nothing," because it may be undermining the very organization that gave it to you, and it may be hurting people farther on down the line.

12

KEEPING IT SIMPLE

Recently I was with a group of Doc students, and they asked me, "Now that we've had our minds and hearts blown open by Doc's teachings, what do we do with our lives?"

He told us, "Live your life like a prayer." That's so beautiful, isn't it? Whatever we are doing, we do it as a prayer. We make it an offering to God, to benefit all of Creation. Dave did his best to put something positive into the world. Even on his deathbed, he was signing books for people yet to come. He dedicated everything he did to the Glory of God and to benefit mankind. So, really, it doesn't matter *what* we do. It matters that we offer it from our heart.

We can't all speak like he did, or write like he did, or tell jokes like he did! I certainly can't do what he did, but I do my best to share his work with others because I've experienced the truth of it. I can speak from my heart and say, "I want to be a better person today" and then dedicate my living for the day as a prayer.

Dave told me, "Just *being* is enough." In his last month, he was physically disabled. His left side was affected by a stroke, so he couldn't get up and walk around. Still, he offered so much to the world in his loving, his kindness, and his prayers. I say that because some of you may be in situations where you can't go out and "do" a lot. It's not about what you do. It's about coming from the heart. "Live your life like a prayer" is about your intention. It's about what's on the inside as you live your day. Dave said, "With a certain level of intention, every moment is expressing the presence of God."

In one of our last video-recorded dialogues, I asked Dave, "As a spiritual teacher, what would you say that real success is?"

> I would, as a spiritual teacher, say that it has to do with fulfilling your obligations to experience the presence of God to the fullest possible extent. And to realize that, as you do this, everything reveals itself as Divinity. As you asked me the question, the Divinity of this moment is revealing itself to me ... the presence of God as the reality of you and I sitting here on this couch speaking at this moment, that is the presence of God.

Dave's teaching is really simple. Everything is the Presence of God. We don't have to go into a cave to find God, or do some grand deed to glorify God. We all carry the light of God inside of us. By living our life like a prayer, we ignite the light of God all around us.

Simple Kindness

I was in the grocery store the other day, and an elderly man was having trouble picking out something. I asked him if I could help him, and he was delighted and grateful that someone noticed he needed a helping hand. I made his day by doing that. No matter how small our kindness may seem to us, it's big to the person we do it for. Maybe it's a smile or a friendly "Hello." At first, maybe you do it because you think, "Oh this is good for my karmic merit ... maybe I'll get something from it." But the more you do it, it's just what you *become*. You become that person who is kind to a stranger or a stray animal, when no one else is looking.

One time, after Dave's lecture, I was standing with a group of women, and they asked me, "What can we do for prosperity?" Prosperity, not posterity, is what they were interested in. They wanted to know how to be prosperous. I told them that they needed to give back. "Give back your time, your effort, your money. Whatever it is that you'd like for yourself, give that to others." I could tell from their faces, they were not expecting me to say that.

I have found it to be very true, that the more we give, the more comes back to us. It's a basic principle: we reap what we sow. There are so many places that need our time and money and caring, whether it's with animals, children, the elderly, or the poor. There are fellow human beings who feel like they can't pull themselves out of a hole, because they have the weight of the world holding them down.

As I get older, I feel especially conscious of the plight of our elderly. I think they should be able to pass into the next world as comfortably as they as can, feeling cared for and valued. They are usually the ones who have given a lot of love and care to everyone else, yet sometimes they are abandoned and left alone when they can't do what they used to. They have good information and wisdom to pass on to us. They are also gracious and knowledgeable about social skills.

Perhaps our older people can help our youth who are so tied to their electronic devices, they don't know how to talk face-to-face very well. The devices may give instant information, but that doesn't mean it is true. In fact, Dave and I calibrated that 50% of information on the internet is under 200. It goes back to what Benjamin Franklin said, "Believe half of what you see." We have to use common sense to distinguish between what is false from what is true.

What I'm saying is that the generations have a lot to learn from each other, but it takes time and patience. Small kindnesses go a long way to healing that generational divide. I was with a friend of mine, and we were in the parking lot of Costco. Here we were, two older women, trying to get a 50-pound bag of dog food into the car. It was not happening! We heard someone say, "Let me help you with that." We turned around to see a young couple walking up to us. The woman was pregnant, and the man was big and strong. He heaved the sack into the car like it was a feather! Their kindness was such a blessing. My friend and I breathed a huge sigh of relief. I was so grateful, I pulled out a $20 bill for them and said, "This is for your baby." They said no, they didn't need the money. I said, "Please, you're blessing me by taking this." That was the truth of it.

A different sort of situation is with the professional beggars. It's a business now in Sedona. You can actually see it. People are brought in vans from out of town, and they are posted up in Sedona, in front of grocery stores, on corners, etc. They beg for a few hours, and then they are picked up in the vans and taken out of town. Another beggar, who operates on her own, was followed by a reporter who did an article on the phenomenon of begging. He noticed that she had a nice apartment down from the road where she was begging. He asked her, "Why do you do this?" She said, "I can get about $300 a day, tax free. Why would I get a job?"

I wondered, *What can I do that is kind but also wise to the overall situation?* So, I talked to a woman who runs a mission that gives food and shelter to people who need it. She told me, "There are people who really do need help. And there are people who are exploiting." She gave me some cards with the information about the mission on it, and sometimes that's what I give to people who are begging. I tell them, "Listen, here's a place where you can get food and they will also give you shelter." Sometimes it's hard to sort out how to do the right thing for people, but I do my best to be kind and I do it from my heart. That way, it's a gift and I let it go.

Recently, I gave a car I'd had for six years to a grandniece. I told her, "If you go to graduate school, I'll give you my car." Basically, I bribed her! She is very smart, and I wanted to encourage her to fulfill her potential; so, I offered her my car if she got into grad school. She was accepted into two outstanding schools. One of my relatives said, "Oh she'll probably just sell the car and keep the money." I said, "That's okay. If she sells the car and takes the money, so be it." It was a gift to her. I was happy to give it to her, free and clear.

When we do things from the heart, that's when it's the most powerful because there are no strings attached. It's not about, "Oh, look what I did—isn't that great of me?!" "I'm earning some good karma with this one!" "Now they owe me." When we share something from our heart—our talent, time, money—then it makes us happy and it makes the other person happy. I'm not sure what my grandniece will do with her life, but it doesn't matter. I'm glad that I was a part of helping her move forward into the next step of her development. No matter what the outcome is, I was able to encourage her and help her along the way. I think that's what we do when we give money to the people who are begging. It's okay whatever we give, whether it's money or a card with helpful information on it. We can't control what people do with what we give them, but we can be kind to everyone we meet. It's like we are seeing our own true Self in everyone.

Have you ever had a magical encounter with a stranger? Recently, I was at lunch with some friends in a little steak house. There was a young man sitting at the bar. As I walked to our booth, I didn't see that he had a service dog lying on the floor and I almost stepped on the dog because he was the same color as the floor. I was observing the man and his dog. Someone walked up to him and said, "Hi, so-and-so, I'm sure glad to see you're out and about today." And I wondered what that meant. I felt very drawn to this man and his dog. I could tell the dog was an amazing creature. He was still and attentive. The waitress brought out the man's bag full of food, which was "to go." He got up to leave. I don't know what compelled me, but I went over to the man and put a $50 bill in his hand, and I said, "Please buy that dog a steak." He looked at me and his face softened. He said, "I have a freezer with steaks in it for him." I said, "You do?!" He said, "Yeah! Look at him. He's huge!" We laughed. And it was true. The dog was almost waist high on me. And I said, "Oh, that's great." And then something magical happened. He gave the dog a command and instantly the dog snapped out of being a service dog and he came up to me in a full-on playful, wagging, love-you-like-crazy doggie love fest. It was just the greatest feeling. This dog went from being a quiet, serious service dog to the most loving wagging dog you could imagine. I looked up from petting the dog into the man's eyes. They were beautiful eyes. I said, "Thank you…" And for that moment, we just looked into each other's eyes. He didn't say a word. I didn't say a word. He snapped his dog back into being a service dog, and they walked out of the restaurant.

I asked the waitress, "Do you know anything about that young man with the service dog?" She said, "Well, I think he was in the military service and his leg got wounded pretty bad." It was just the way he looked at me and I looked at him and said thank you. Not another word took place. I still remember the feeling. It was one of those moments when you know the light ignited inside. Like Dave said, the presence of God is in everything, and all we have to do is notice it. At our most recent virtual gathering, we read this quote from Dave:

> Simple kindness to oneself and all that lives is the most power-ful transformational force of all. It produces no backlash and has no downside. It never leads to loss or despair. True kind-ness, simple kindness increases one's own true power without exacting any toll….To reach maximum power, such kindness can permit no exception. Nor can it be practiced with the ex-pectation of some selfish gain or reward. Every kindness is forever.

This reminds me of a man in India who is called "the forest man of India." Forty years ago, he noticed that the area near him had become a desert wasteland. There was no green left, and no animals that lived there anymore. He began planting trees. Day after day, he planted a tree on this desert sandbar, and he did this for decades. He would take clippings from the trees in his yard, and carry them for miles to this desert area, plant them in the soil there, and water them. This man had three children, and he lived in what might be considered a slum. He walked a long way each time to plant the trees on the sandbar. Now, forty years later, the area is named after him, the Molai Forest, a flourishing forest of 1,300 acres. Wild animals have returned—deer, tigers, many species of birds, and even a herd of one hundred elephants who have birthed their calves in the forest.

That's an example of how one person can change everything, through one simple kindness each day. I encourage you to decide on something you really care about. And then do it with that same love, care, and constancy.

Recently someone has helped this "forest man" write a book about it, and films have been made about his forest. He is a simple man who did it out of love for the earth and mankind. He wasn't seeking fame. No one even knew about him for decades. He is using his fame now to bring attention to the children. He would like for the education system to teach children how to plant trees and how to take care of the earth. He teaches children how to plant a single tree and take care of it. He believes this simple practice of caring for another living being will help children become a certain quality of person.

True greatness is an *inner* quality. And it begins with the small steps before we can take giant steps. Some people come into Dave's work and they read about enlightenment and that's the giant goal they set for themselves. That's a wonderful goal and is our destiny in some lifetime. But let's not forget that Dave said the path begins with "kindness in everyday life." I don't think we can skip over that step! In order to reach a giant goal, like enlightenment, we have to develop the inner qualities we need, such as being a kind person, being a determined person, being a forgiving person. The enlightened beings are very few. I feel like I'm doing enough just trying to be kind and spreading the light in my little corner of the universe. Mother Teresa said to do "small things with great love."

Dave taught that basic kindness to others plays a major role in daily life and spiritual progress. For instance, if your neighbor is ill or had surgery, see if you can take out the garbage cans or bring them some groceries. If you see an old lady having trouble with her grocery cart, let her go in front of you. Maybe she's tired of standing. Be kind to the pregnant mom with a screaming kid in her cart. Instead of giving her a dirty look and judging her as a "bad mother," let her go in front of you. What's ten more minutes? If your goal is to evolve spiritually, then kindness is a vital tool.

Caring for the Children

Something beautiful is to see children being kind to other children. A few years ago, I went on a trip with my daughter and granddaughter to the beach. When we got to the beach, my granddaughter saw a group of other kids putting sand on a little boy's legs, and he was loving it. But then the kids got bored and wandered off, leaving the boy alone. So, when my granddaughter saw this, she went over to play with him. She put sand on his legs, and he was so happy. She liked making him happy. He looked up at her and gave her the most beautiful smile. They were laughing and having a great time. We found out that the boy has spina bifida, and he could not move. His mother had carried him up and down the hill to get to the beach. He loved the ocean, and he also loved the interaction with the other children too, but it was hard because he could not move. He could only sit on the sand. He and my granddaughter were the same age, five. She could tell something was different about him, but she didn't care. They had a fun time playing together.

As we were walking back up to our car, my daughter was appreciating my granddaughter and how she had played with the little boy. "He was laughing and having fun with you. That was really wonderful. I'm proud of you for being kind and making a new friend." It melted my heart to hear my daughter encouraging her daughter to be kind. I was thinking, *This is what it's all about. It's not about how much money you make, it's not about what you can do for your kids materialistically. It's not about how many degrees they have. The important thing is to teach them to be decent, caring, kind human beings, and for them to pass that along to the next generation.*

So, as parents, I think that's one of our greatest contributions—to teach our children kindness, compassion, and to have a willingness to take that extra step for people who have any kind of difficulty, no matter what it is, whether it is health, loneliness, or just not being able to pull things out of the grocery cart. We can take the items out of the cart for a little old lady or man and put them onto the checkout belt. If we see someone struggling, we can lend a hand or smile or kind word.

Dave was concerned about the violence that children are exposed to. He talked to me about it often. He could see the visceral impact of video games, movies, rap music, and even animated cartoons, and how negative they are. He said these media alter the brain and the psyche, through entrainment to negativity. The violence and negativity actually get wired into children. When children see violence on a screen, it engenders violence. Video games desensitize them to attacking, killing and death. He was very much against violence on the screen, because he said that it directly affects the brain function and consciousness, especially of children and young people. He said it actually "programs" them into becoming violent. Even if it's a video "game," and it's in a Viking setting or costume, it's still entraining the brains into tearing down, killing, attacking, torturing, etc. It teaches our children that being mean, cutting others down, and violence are acceptable modes of thinking and acting.

Parents, grandparents and guardians are responsible for what our children are watching on television, the internet, and so forth. We need to take the responsibility to teach love, caring, and compassion to children, that is, to give them environments where they are exposed to spiritual lessons, not violence. I know that it's hard on parents, because of holding down jobs and dealing with personal problems, but it's so important to be aware of what children are watching and to keep them protected from negative programs as long as possible. It doesn't mean they have to watch programs on sainthood or something super-spiritual! It's more about quality time with the children, giving them freedom to come to know what their natural talents are before they are programmed by media. It's wonderful to take them outdoors, teach them how to be kind to animals, or how to plant a garden. Those are the things that nourish the souls of children.

Dave was not surprised by the upsurge of mass shootings and school shootings. My daughter is a teacher, and she tells me that more and more teachers are quitting or changing jobs because it's getting too violent. She had to take a training on what to do if her school was attacked. Just think of that! The place where children are supposed to be educated, mentored, cared for—and now it's one of the most dangerous places for them to be. Violence has permeated our culture, and Dave said it is because of the "entertainment" industry which is actually "entraining" the collective consciousness to violence.

It is very troubling, yet we can't swim around in the soup of despair over where the world is going. We have to be creative with our humor and come up with some light-nourishing measures. Dave and I shared a strange sense of humor, so I will tell you something that's in that category. I'm using violence in the media to lose weight. Yes, you read that correctly. It's called the "Susan Hawkins diet." Here's what you do. Go and rent one of the worst horrible, bloody movies you can think of. Get it set up on your television. Now fix yourself a great big plate of food and sit down in front of your television. Turn on that awful movie, and I guarantee it will make you sick and you'll only eat half of what's on your plate!

There are plenty of truly nourishing things for our children and for our own souls. Often, they are simple and free of charge. One of the favorite ways to nourish my soul is to walk in the local Buddhist Stupa garden.

Prayer

In our day and age, it's very hard to find moments of peace and prayer with the electronics everywhere we turn. It's a common scene in homes now for every member of the family to have their face stuck to a device. Instead of talking or playing together, each person is on their device. I like my devices too. They are incredibly handy. I can do all my coupons for the grocery store right there

on my smart phone. It's hard to pull ourselves away from the electronics, but if we can, then that's when we will see the miracles of
life all around us.

A couple of years ago, I went with a friend to a retreat at a
monastery where they had a silent breakfast. My friend and I knew
we needed to sit at separate tables in the dining hall, because we
have a tendency to get each other giggling. And, so, I was sitting by
myself at one of the tables, looking out the window. The silence
gave me time to reflect. There were several people around me, but
we were all silent. As I looked out the window, I saw a dead tree
off to the left. I thought, *Why don't they just take that dead tree out?
Everything around it is green and colorful.* When I went deeper into seeing it, I noticed how actually alive it was, because many different
birds were resting in it. They obviously loved being in that dead
tree. Life was vibrant in and around the tree. And in the middle
of this magical scene, I noticed a century plant that was growing. I
didn't see it when I first looked out, but there it was looking at us
through the window.

We nurture our soul when we take time to reflect on our sur-
roundings. We see and hear the expressions of life around us, and
then our own inner light is ignited. Starting off the day like that,
with some silent reflection, gives time to reflect on our own spiritual self. It sets the tone for the whole day. Even if we only do it
for ten minutes a day, a lot of insight can come.

Dave was always dropping down into that quiet space in order
to reflect. Sometimes he called it a nap! He would go lie down for
a short nap after lunch. If I had time, I would go lie down with
him. It was a quiet time that we both found restful and soulful. So
whatever works in your day, see if you can find that regular time
for silent reflection, even if it's just ten minutes a day.

Contemplation is something Dave did all the time. When I
knew him, he didn't do formal meditation; he did contemplation. As you probably know from his books and lectures, he talked about the difference between meditation and contemplation.
He said meditation can be helpful. You learn how to focus your

attention and go within to explore various inner states. For many decades, he meditated for an hour in the morning and an hour in the evening. But, Dave said, meditation has limited value because it is compartmentalized from the rest of your life, so he recommended contemplation. I saw him do this, nonstop. Whatever he was doing, he had an inner awareness of God in the background. I would see him sit quietly, inwardly contemplating. Sometimes, he was praying about something that he wanted an answer to, maybe a problem. The answer would always come within a day or so. It's like his inner being embodied Psalm 91: "I will say of the Lord, He is my refuge and my fortress; my God, in Him will I trust." Psalm 91 is a chapter in the Bible that he used often for his contemplative life. He would take one verse, a month at a time, and allow it to infuse his being.

The world is very serious and loud. It's easy to get caught up in all the drama of politics and the endless negativities in the news. Lately it seems that all we hear about are catastrophes and crises. The news tells us everything that's wrong in the world. What do we do with that constant "bad news"? Instead of getting caught up in the drama, we can say a prayer that the leaders make the right decision, and we can say a prayer for the people who are suffering. Prayer is a powerful way to be present with the suffering of the world.

Dave taught us to pray in such a way that we surrender the person or the situation to God. That's different than how many people learned to pray when they were children, which was to tell God what you want to happen. We hear these prayers in churches. People dictate to God, "Please do this, heal this, bless this, solve this." I learned from Dave that we can help a person and a situation a lot by simply remembering them in our prayer. He didn't dictate to God what to do. He taught me to pray like this: state the problem, open up about what you need help with, pray from your heart, and then surrender it to God. Sometimes God answers us in a way that we don't expect or even want! But when you get older and look back on what would have happened, you realize that God answered in the way that was best for you. There are many things I wanted when I was younger that I am now glad I didn't get!

When Dave and I lost something around the house, he would say a prayer about finding the object and then he would let it go. Suddenly the object would appear. It might be an important paper we had to sign, for example. You know how that goes. You put it in a safe place, and then you forget where you put it. Dave would pray about it, then let it go. About five minutes later, we'd find whatever it was we were looking for. He was very good about praying and then letting it go. That's the hard part! A lot of us pray, but then we don't let go. Surrendering what we want out of it is the most important part of any spiritual practice.

When praying for others, Dave taught us to pray for the "highest good" and not a specific outcome. That way, we're aligning our prayer with the higher destiny of their soul. We don't know what the karma of the situation might be. Only God knows. We don't know what the soul might be going through, or needing to learn, from that situation. We don't know the higher purpose of it for that person and for the people around them. But we can pray for their highest good, out of our love for them, and that absolutely brings the light of God's grace to help them.

Questions and Answers

Q: I don't have a question. I'm just so grateful. My whole life has been changed by Doc's teachings. What can I do to express my gratitude? I'm so grateful for every single thing that you and Doc have done. I traveled to this event from another country just so I could be here in this energy.

A: Your heart is open right now because of all the energy that you're receiving. I can tell it's really impacting you. I think that once you go back home, you'll carry this energy with you, from here on out. And what you need to do will come to you. Give it time. Whether it's in your own personal life, to show gratitude, or whether it's starting a study group, or whatever you would like to do.

A lot of us here have been where you are, and we understand. I want to tell you that this energy, you'll carry it with you in your aura, just like you carry the teachings that he taught, in your aura. All of us do, because it's a true teaching. So, when you go home, it will come to you what is right for you to do. And if you need any help, you can email us and we will talk with you about it. Study groups are good. Talking to people about the work is good, but pick your settings. Use discernment. Doc's work has changed many people's lives, just like it changed yours. Pray about it, then the answers come in due time.

Q: What are some of the predictions that Doc made twenty years ago that you see are coming true?

A: I often tell people about his prediction on the impact of video games and violent media. He nailed that one in *Power vs Force*. It's unbelievable how many school shootings there are, even at an elementary school, but Dave would not have been surprised at all. He and I talked about it a lot. He was very concerned about the prevalence of video games and violence occurring everywhere you look on television, even in cartoons.

His book *Truth vs. Falsehood* laid out the dynamics that are now happening in terms of world politics, and the decline of Western civilization. He wrote that book in 2003, and we see it happening now, almost twenty years later.

In another prediction, he said that commercials would sell 10 times more of their product if an animal was in the commercial. Well, look, almost every commercial you see now has some kind of animal. It's not just to sell dog food or cat food. It's to sell whatever they're talking about. It's because people have a place in their heart for animals, and so it gets people in that good feeling warm space, and then they buy the product. I myself pay closer attention to an ad if there are animals in it.

Q: Did Doc talk about being kind to oneself?

A: "Kindness to all of life, including yourself," is how he put it.

Dave grew up in a religious environment that taught guilt for a sinful thought, like you had a spot on your soul. That's the background of many people. But Dave's teachings are about compassion for yourself as a human being, not beating yourself up for a mistake. He liked to say, "Be your own best friend." That's a way of saying, "Be kind to yourself." Dave was a hard worker, but he also knew how to play. He taught us to have "balance" in our lives. He liked relaxing with the dog and playing with the kitties. We had so much fun just watching the three kitties play around in the living room. If the kitties got anywhere near her bone, the dog, Kelsey, would growl. It was a fun little circus we had in our living room, and Dave loved just sitting there and being with the animals. So, Dave was kind to himself, yes. It's because he enjoyed all of life. He liked to have fun and laugh. And he also liked to work hard at what he was doing so he felt good about his effort to serve God and help others. Kindness to yourself is related to kindness to others. They go hand in hand.

Q: The world seems to be going in a bad direction right now. Do you worry about the future?

A: No, because Dave said consciousness is always evolving. Things are always changing. Creation and destruction are both innate to the circle of life. Civilizations come and go, but consciousness is always evolving.

I have a pendant that is the Ying and Yang. The white and the black intertwine to make a circle. One cannot exist without the other. Together, they make a whole. I want to say that the world is perfectly balanced between light and dark. Neither one can overcome the other. So as long as you understand that, there's no fear of the future, because the future is always within the circle.

Look at this Covid-19 pandemic that occurred out of nowhere and shut the whole world down! Even as businesses and schools are opening back up, we won't go back to what it was. A virus is a negative thing in that it has killed so many people, yet something new has come out of it.

I think it's important to look back on our lives and know that whenever we have difficult times, when we think that we're in the dark, there's always the light that is there to guide us. And it's important to us as people and as students of Doc's work, that we realize that we do not have to fear or feel hopeless. There may be hard times, but there's always the light that will guide us out of it. When I look at the world, I see that there's a purpose to what is happening, and that each of us has a purpose here, which is to be kind to others and to be respectful of life.

Q: One of my favorite things about Doc was when he did his OM in a lecture.
A: I still hear his OM. It was the longest and lowest OM, wasn't it? He could hold it longer than anyone I've ever heard. I could not believe it. It was just amazing. And here he was in his eighties, and he was able to hold it that long. Everyone would say, "Doc, please do your OM," because it was of that higher calibration, and it took us to that higher speechless space.

We should be grateful that he was here on earth with us and that we were able to be in his presence and hear him. He was like an angel among us. He was so extraordinary. He brought us all together as a flock. Remember he said that, as a spiritual group, we all swoop in together, and we all swoop out together. We were blessed because he gave us a core that we will always carry in our inner person, from lifetime to lifetime. If we don't make it to enlightenment this lifetime, we will make it sometime because we have that energy in our souls that we carry, and we have all the teachings that he left us. He worked hard to do the lectures and make sure that he had answered any question that would come up after he was gone. He left us with this whole body of material, so that if we have a question, we just have to refer to the material. Of course, he buried the answer in 250 lectures, but you'll find it in there somewhere!

Q: What is your advice to people who did not get to physically meet Dr. Hawkins, but have come across as writings and would like to be a student of his?

A: What's my advice? Do the work, follow the teachings to the best of your ability, with devotion in your heart to the Truth, and earn the merit to meet the teacher you're supposed to meet. It isn't about the person. It's about the teachings and learning from those. So maybe your karmic destiny is to meet another teacher in person that's better for you at this time. I think Doc's work is preparing you for perhaps another time in this life or another lifetime.

Q: Which book do you recommend for a beginner to start learning from Doc?

A: It depends on the person. I would recommend *Letting Go* for someone who is looking to build a solid spiritual foundation. If they have done a lot of spiritual work, then I recommend *Power versus Force*, then for them to go to *Eye of the I*, and then *I: Reality and Subjectivity,* which is very advanced. A lot of people go on and on about *I*, and maybe they think they understand it, but of course they do not. Those are the three books he started out writing as a trilogy. *Eye of the I* is one of my favorite books, because it has so many of the inner workings that all of us need to know, and also *Letting Go,* because we can't do the work until we let go of the past. Once we let go the past, heal something in our psychology, then we're ready to focus on our spirituality. Before recommending a book, I always feel someone out first as to how much work they've already done on themselves and what would be most suitable for them at this time. And there are his other books such as *Healing and Recovery,* which he did way back in the early 80s, but it's still powerful for today. That book came from his video series on healing, in all facets of life: illness, anxiety, depression, sexuality, addiction, cancer, etc. These video programs are the archival "Office Series," and he did them wearing a little bow tie. That was thirty years ago, or more. So, he devoted his entire life to his own spiritual advancement as well as ours. I don't know anything else that a spiritual teacher can give us as a gift other than that.

Q: What it was like to be so close to Doc for such long periods of time?
A: Just like being with yourself. Where I began and he left off, there was no difference. We could be together whether we were together physically or not. That way, whenever we were apart, we were still together. It was like that from the beginning. We just clicked.

Q: In *Truth versus Falsehood*, the Ganges River calibrates at around 500 and then you and Doc calibrated the river at an event, and it went up to 700. What was the reason for the 200-point discrepancy?
A: It could have been that some avatar who was very high had passed, and the ashes were thrown into the Ganges. I am just guessing. It didn't go down, so that's good! There are a lot of things like that which change, and it would take a while to research the exact reasons for it.

Q: What was one of the last things that you and Doc did together?
A: The last few months he wasn't getting out much. He liked staying home. But he decided he would like to go to the Ash Wednesday service at the church. Even though he was not into religiousness, Dave appreciated the sacraments of the church. "Ashes to ashes and dust to dust." He said, "That's something to contemplate, isn't it?" Looking back on it, maybe he knew he didn't have much longer. "You and I are both going to become ashes someday, sweetheart," he said. I have a picture of Dave and me with the ashes on our foreheads from that service. And then of course I told him a funny joke: "Honey, you've never seen a U-Haul following a hearse, have you?" He laughed and laughed. And, so, wherever he is now, he is free. There's no U-Haul and no earthly baggage. "Ashes to ashes and dust to dust." He did everything he needed to do here on earth, and then he was free to leave it. I'm so grateful he was here and that we all got to be with him. His body is ash, but his Spirit is everywhere.

EPILOGUE

I want to thank you for reading this book. I hope it is helpful to you. Maybe it gives you a better understanding of who and what Dave was. You have his books and his public lectures. And now you have this book, which shares with you what he was like "behind the scenes." A lot of people are one way in public and another way at home, but not Dave. He was the same kind, wise, funny, and loving man, whether he was on stage or at home.

He was an extraordinary person. It would be easy for all of us to focus on him as a personality, but he told us not to do that. He pointed us to the Divinity of the Self within. He told us to respect the teacher, not to deify him. I think he would be happiest if we honored him by living the teachings and "becoming" that which we truly are.

Dave gave us the gift of a spiritual path that we can follow in the midst of an ordinary human life. We don't have to join anything, adopt a prescribed "spiritual" lifestyle, take vows, or set ourselves apart from others. God is in *all* things. Remember how he saw the beauty of the trash can in the alleyway? The path, he said, is to live with care and kindness in everyday life, because that's where God is present—in everything around us. As he wrote in *Power vs. Force*, "... just being ordinary is an expression of Divinity; the truth of one's real Self can be discovered in the pathway of everyday life. To live with care and kindness is all that is necessary; the rest reveals itself in due time. The commonplace and God are not distinct."

We all have a light inside, and it's up to us to brighten it and shine it. That's what Dave and I have tried to do. We have done our best to become what we were meant to become, and to benefit the spiritual advancement of everyone around us. I encourage you and bless you to nourish the light of your own soul and to shine it wherever you are.

APPENDIX

Map of Consciousness®

God-view	Life-view	Level		Log	Emotion	Process
Self	Is	Enlightenment	⇧	700-1000	Ineffable	Pure Consciousness
All-Being	Perfect	Peace	⇧	600	Bliss	Illumination
One	Complete	Joy	⇧	540	Serenity	Transfiguration
Loving	Benign	Love	⇧	500	Reverence	Revelation
Wise	Meaningful	Reason	⇧	400	Understanding	Abstraction
Merciful	Harmonious	Acceptance	⇧	350	Forgiveness	Transcendence
Inspiring	Hopeful	Willingness	⇧	310	Optimism	Intention
Enabling	Satisfactory	Neutrality	⇧	250	Trust	Release
Permitting	Feasible	Courage	⇕	200	Affirmation	Empowerment
Indifferent	Demanding	Pride	⇩	175	Scorn	Inflation
Vengeful	Antagonistic	Anger	⇩	150	Hate	Aggression
Denying	Disappointing	Desire	⇩	125	Craving	Enslavement
Punitive	Frightening	Fear	⇩	100	Anxiety	Withdrawal
Disdainful	Tragic	Grief	⇩	75	Regret	Despondency
Condemning	Hopeless	Apathy	⇩	50	Despair	Abdication
Vindictive	Evil	Guilt	⇩	30	Blame	Destruction
Despising	Miserable	Shame	⇩	20	Humiliation	Elimination

ABOUT THE AUTHOR

Susan Hawkins serves as president of The Institute for Spiritual Research, Inc., the foundation started by her husband, Dr. David R. Hawkins (d. 2012). He said she was the "fulcrum" that made possible the sharing of his knowledge and presence in the world. He pointed to her keen intuition, personal warmth, and crucial companionship. She always traveled with him during his years of public teaching, and he was never onstage without her. She joined him in several video-recorded dialogues on practical topics such as "Improving Your Relationships" and "Live Your Life Like a Prayer." After his passing in 2012, she continued to hold a yearly gathering in Sedona, Arizona, until 2019, when she began offering regular virtual gatherings for inspiration and fellowship. For more information on her events, to contact her, or to sign up for their newsletter, go to the website for Veritas Publishing: www.veritas-pub.com

Printed in the USA
CPSIA information can be obtained
at www.ICGtesting.com
LVHW040556261024
794811LV00042B/745